Parent Prerogatives

How to Handle
Teacher-Misbehaviors
and Other School Disorders

Parent Prerogatives

How to Handle Teacher-Misbehaviors and Other School Disorders

Richard L. Weinberg
& Lynn Goetsch Weinberg

Nelson-Hall **nh** Chicago

Library of Congress Cataloging in Publication Data
Weinberg, Richard L.
  Parent prerogatives.

  Includes index.
  1. Parent-teacher relationships. 2. Home and school.
I. Weinberg, Lynn Goetsch, joint author. II. Title.
LC225.W38   371.1'03   78-23718
ISBN 0-88229-442-3

Manufactured in the United States of America

10 9 8 7 6 5 4 3 2 1

To our parents, our children,
and to three outstanding educators,
Doris, Peg, and Kirsten.

Contents

Preface

Every child has school problems from time to time, sometimes serious problems which cry for parental help. Yet, most parents feel totally helpless and inadequate in attempting to help their child solve even minor school problems, let alone major problems. Parents are sadly lacking information and are needlessly baffled by the school system, the theories, the philosophies, the double-talk, and jargon used by educators.

Teachers and administrators treat parents condescendingly or with contempt, handling the parents as they handle the child, high-handedly manipulating them out of their rights. Intellectually inferior, militant teachers have a ready arsenal for intimidating children and parents alike, in order to conceal teacher-misbehavior and academic incompetency. This intimidation is intentional because of the educators' own concealed fears that parents might discover how inadequate teachers and schools are.

Parents must overcome their own teacher-phobia in order to protect their children. Parents must learn how to assert their legal prerogatives to protect the next generation which is direly threatened by a rapidly deterio-

ix

rating educational system. To do this, parents need facts that only educator-parents from within the system can give them.

This is not a book for educators; it is written in conversational, question-and-answer, layman's language, for parents, future parents, grandparents, and all others who have long felt that the schools are a "disaster area." Good educators will applaud the ideas presented in this volume, but other educators will consider the book a personal threat to them if parents follow even some of the suggestions.

Parent Prerogatives provides parents with specific "how-to" techniques for handling particular school problems on an individual basis. Sample conversations between parents and teachers, such as Mr. Mark E. Desade and Ms. Dee Tention, illustrate the use of "Parental Persistence" to obtain specific goals which immediately pressure the school to meet more adequately Johnnie's and Suzie's needs. The book informs parents of recent attitudinal and academic deterioration as well as traditional teacher tactics for handling both parents and children; it is a compendium of solutions for differing types of school problems which arise many times throughout the schooling years.

Individual, "now," parental intervention techniques presented in *Parent Prerogatives* differentiate it from other books concerning America's schools. Other books suggest that parents trust the educators and cooperate their children and themselves out of appropriate and adequate education, or they suggest only that parents join a parent group to work for changes within the system. Indirect, group action, which is also needed, does not alleviate the personal hell a child is experiencing today. *Parent Prerogatives* gives parents a sense of personal control over the schooling of their children and a sense of adequacy in helping a child now—today, when the child needs protection and help to realize his potential as a person and a worthwhile, contributing member of society.

1

It's Your Move

You Too?

Welcome to the crowd. So you too are not completely happy with the schools? What are you dissatisfied about? Maybe your Suzie is not learning to read as she should? Is her understanding of arithmetic far behind what it should be? Why is that? You don't know? You're baffled because you, after all, are not a teacher and you don't understand those things?

Or maybe Johnnie is doing OK work, but he doesn't like school? He used to be such a delightfully curious boy and enjoyed learning—but now he has turned off? Is he a highly intelligent boy who drags himself to school as though he were being punished? Maybe he is. Maybe he is being punished by inadequate, incompetent, uninterested or brutal teachers.

You have serious doubts about the teacher's ability, maybe even about her basic intelligence? Does she evade your questions and resort to educational cliches, "you

1

knows" and other gobbledegook which cause you to consider talking with her a lost cause? Do you wonder if her evasive manner and double-talk are cover-ups for ignorance and stupidity—hers, not yours?

Are you fed up with the school? You've had big trouble? What kind? Has a teacher been slapping or battering your child, or merely harassing him—calling him cruel names? Has an unscrupulous teacher threatened or humiliated your child to the point that he now goes to school petrified of the next onslaught? Does a Ms. Sneer treat your Suzie with such a "put-down" attitude that Suzie too has begun sneering at any mention of school?

Worse than that, is it? Has the whole school staff ganged up on Johnnie and "has it in for him"? You mean the kid hates school, the school hates him—they want to get rid of him? And you'd like to be rid of them? Have they told you that Johnnie is everything but good? And have they told you his difficulties are a result of your mismanagement? Have they built a case against him to the point that he has no chance? Is it like trying to appease a tiger that is intent on devouring you?

Well, what are you going to do about it? Nothing? Is that fair to your child? You'd like to do something about it, but you don't know how, you say?

If you find yourself seeking answers to any of these questions, read on. That is what this book is about—proposing answers to parents for some of those frustrating school problems. And we are not going to give you any of the usual pap or platitudes that most books dish out to parents. We know where you are—because we've been there!

Not only have we been where you are, but we've also been on the other side of the desk—the teacher's side of the desk. We know that all teachers are not angels and that schools can be a living hell for many children. No, you're not alone; you have lots of company.

Parents Have Rights Too!

As teachers, trainer-of-teachers, and parents, we have witnessed and experienced the child-defeating strategies, the stupidity, the cover-up philosophies, the abuse of theories and methods, the double-talk jargon, the conniving and the bamboozling. We intend to cut through all the verbal garbage the schools and most books dispense to parents, and give you some straight answers, practical suggestions and strategies to use so that you can do something about the school's improper treatment of your child —*if* you choose to help your child. It is high time that someone from within the educational profession shattered some of the myths to parents and "gave them their rights."

Most parents are not privy to what really goes on in the schools, the teacher misbehaviors, the humiliation of children, and the ignorant or stupid nonteaching in the classroom, the sanctimonious and vicious attitudes, and slanderous and libelous conversations that take place in the faculty lounge and lunchroom. What goes on in those places, concealed from parents, is very different from the pose, the professional mask, that teachers and administrators present to the public. Let's strip away the mask and see what is behind it.

Let Us Service You Better

Whenever I hear the expression, "We want to service you better," whether it comes from the public utility companies or the public schools, I think of the docile cow. Raised in an agricultural area, I learned very early what "servicing" meant. It was the politesse used by cattle breeders as the euphemism for what the bull does to the docile cow to produce a baby cow. And today, a "screwing" can be something quite contrary to the enjoyment of sex.

Stop Being So Damn Docile

You must be your child's advocate because nobody else will be. Although educators will give profuse lip-service to their "deep" concern for Suzie, and will talk you to death about their "herculean" efforts to help *all* the children, the truth of the matter is that many educators are self-servicing SOBs, not child-serving. Their only herculean efforts are devoted to making their job as easy as they can and to making sure they keep their jobs.

Teacher militancy today speaks this message loud and clear. Newspapers daily proclaim teacher demands, union threats, and teacher walkouts. Teachers are interested in working conditions, including stronger authority over your children, salary increases, fringe benefits, and job security. Teachers' unions are getting stronger as administrators and school boards get weaker. In this battle between management and labor, your children get caught in the middle with no rights and no one to represent them, except *you*.

Ultimately, the responsibility for protecting the children rests with the parents. If more parents personally and individually protected their own child whenever a problem arose, then all children would have better protection. Everybody else in education is "surviving," so you better see to it that your child survives. Most of the problems take place at the classroom level or start there and grow worse, and it is at this level that you must start working.

The Power Is Yours

Legally, you have the power to act *now*. Control of the schools legally rests in your hands if you will only use your power. The only power the schools have is that which you have given them. Default of parental power has allowed the schools to become the stifling, brutal institutions they are. By failing to exercise your power, your children are suffering in the hands of a profession that is rapidly becoming more and more tyrannical.

For all too long, teachers' own inadequacies have caused them to resort to misbehaviors. You as parents must learn techniques for recognizing and handling school problems in such a way that the teacher is forced to learn better methods of handling her job. The bad teacher will learn new methods and behavior only if she is taught that she can no longer get away with mishandling your child and you in her efforts to cover up her own job-bungling. These misfits who cannot learn new methods and cannot cope with your demands for proper handling of Johnnie and Suzie must be forced to find a new profession.

The local school board is legally responsible for the way educators perform, but the board does not do a very good job of this. And you could not wait long enough for the requisite change even if the attempt were being made. School boards are burdened down with bureaucracy and finances. As in all other arenas of representative government, the public knows that working through the bureaucracy is at best extremely slow and at worst hopelessly doomed before it starts. Your child needs help *now*—from you, personally and individually.

All parents know that when they have a problem at home with their child, they have to handle it now—on the spot. You cannot wait for six months or a year to have a broken leg set and put into a cast. The same is true for handling school problems. You must handle it now—on the spot, before the problem develops into a bigger one.

"Parental Persistence"

Parents have abdicated their control of the schools because of three basic mistakes: the first of these is that parents place too much trust in teachers and schools, assuming that the teachers know what they are doing, will do it correctly, and will treat Johnnie and Suzie with human fairness. T'aint so. Some teachers deserve this trust;

many do not. The second mistake is that parents take a do-nothing attitude. Or they make a feeble attempt to correct a problem and then revert to doing nothing, considering the situation hopeless or impossible. This kind of running from the problem results from parental fears—fear of worsening the situation, fear of losing, fear of not being liked, and fear of appearing ignorant or stupid. These fears are "your stuff" which the schools use against you and your child. Getting angry and doing nothing is the third mistake, or getting angry and lashing out at the teacher. Venting your anger might make you temporarily feel better, but it does not solve the problem for Johnnie or Suzie.

Johnnie would like to fight or else run from the situation also, but he cannot. He is stuck with it, both physically and mentally, living with it day in and day out. Maybe Johnnie can cope with it and maybe he cannot. If he cannot cope with a bad school situation, you will have more than school problems on your hands.

You probably feel guilty about your inability to help your child—and you should. Because there are things you can do to help. Even if Suzie can cope with a bad situation, why should she? Although she copes beautifully, Suzie's learning will be hindered, and she will be developing some very bad feelings about life, learning, school in particular, and maybe even you for your weaknesses in not being able to do something to correct her situation.

O.K., Smartass, how do I handle this? There are alternative methods for asserting your parental power in the school. First, let's dispense quickly with the first two methods, which you already know, and get on to "Parental Persistence" procedures which are expanded further with specific examples in other chapters.

The first method, chatting with the teacher on a friendly, cooperative basis, most parents have used with varying lack of success. It is always worth a try, and it is beautiful—if it works, but it often does not work. You are reading this, aren't you? The second level—complaining to the principal to pressure a teacher—is often not very effective today because of weak administrators and rising teacher-militancy. After these two approaches fail, most parents quit—unfortunately for their children. There are better methods.

The Three Bears

Get on familiar terms with the three bears so they can help you understand and use "Parental Persistence":
1. Bear down on school personnel to obtain your specific goal.
2. Bear insults and intimidations without anger, fear, or fighting.
3. Bear with the problem as long as it takes to attain your goal—don't run.

You must know exactly what you want changed and refuse to allow the school personnel to divert you from that goal. Don't let educators channel the discussion away from your goal onto "safer waters"—safer for them. Don't let them jolly you and assure you that everything is "peachy-keen." Repeat, repeat, and then repeat again what you want changed. The school will try its best not to hear your request or any request they don't want to fulfill. Don't be afraid to sound like a stuck record.

If you get angry or the teachers are able to provoke you to anger, you will have lost your ability to use your clear thinking to deal with them. Your anger will also be turned against you by the teachers. They can then do their "Poor, Poor Me" act—for having to deal with those "horrible" people. Or they will discount you and your complaint with self-righteous indignation, exemplified by, "It's no wonder Johnnie is such a monster—with parents like that." Don't give Ms. Ella Mentary and Mr. Mani Pulator an excuse for continuing their bad behavior. If you are angry, use it to accomplish your goal, but don't allow yourself the luxury of an emotional blasting off.

If you run from the situation without ever dealing with it, you have lost before you started, obviously. Too many parents make a timid, tentative or wishful request to a teacher or administrator and are soft-soaped or otherwise handled out of their request. Don't run from the school, feeling dissatisfied or confused. Don't give up so easily. Don't let them wear you out; *you* wear *them* out. Bear with it until you get the job done.

Teachers and administrators capitalize on parents' basic fear of school authority figures. Educators state their opinions as though those opinions were gospel, and they try to ignore what you say as they rudely interrupt you to out-talk you. This manifestation of what I call the educators' social disease is partly their practiced act in dealing with children, and it is partly their defense against you. You should remember that teachers are every bit as afraid of you as you are of them. It is a teacher's business to handle parents; they are experienced pros at it. You must learn to be more persistent than they are!

If you give up and flee from the problem, you will have doomed your child to putting up with the problem because of your cowardice. The educators can then sit back and congratulate themselves on how well they handled you. Even though their authoritarian act has been apparently successful, a corner of their mind continues to worry about it and hopes you have quit. Don't!

One Thing at a Time

Parental Persistence should be applied individually to one specific goal at a time. You must have your goal specifically in mind and not let the school off the hook until it has satisfied you on that issue. Whatever your goal, you must cling to that single purpose with bulldog tenacity. Do not let the school change the subject and divert you from that goal. Only in this way can you force the schools to assume their responsibilities to your child.

Remember, if you quit the game short of winning your point, *you* are failing your child. You have state school laws on your side. You have federal laws and court decisions on your side. You also have professional ethics and the educators' natural fear of criticism working for you. All you have to do is to use all this. It's your move.

2

Teacher-Misbehavior

Polishing Rotten Apples Produces Vinegar

The traditional consideration of all teachers as "perfect" has been a very comfortable position for teachers, and they have conspired to perpetuate the myth. The school places the onus on the child to conform and perform, according to the dictates of the teacher. If a child has problems, the child is at fault—never the teacher. The teacher's behavior is never questioned. If all teachers were intelligent, fair and just, this attitude might be correct. But it is high time that teacher-behavior should be questioned because very few teachers are models of perfection, exuding honesty, fairness and justice. Teacher-misbehavior is the causative agent for many, if not most, school problems.

Court conflicts raging between the public schools and the American Civil Liberties Union representing students have revealed that the conflict has been oversimplified, reduced to an either-or situation. Either the teachers are given ironfisted control of the students or the students are given total control, creating anarchy in the schools. As the legal battles are fought in the courts, all attention has been focused on resolution of student-misbehavior. Teacher-misbehavior is not even considered as the causal factor of the original problem. This legalistic approach is the natural outgrowth of the basic problem, teacher-misbehavior; this approach is tantamount to using Band-Aids for a ruptured appendix instead of surgery.

The full-grown adolescent will not tolerate the teacher-misbehavior that the helpless elementary-child must tolerate. In fact, the unquestioned teacher-misbehavior that children have experienced in the elementary schools has largely created the physical confrontations between students and teachers at the high-school level, and thus the entrance of the American Civil Liberties Union and court battles.

Typically, the schools attribute the students' bad behavior to the parents and the home. In some cases this may be true, but the bulk of the school's problems are created right in the school by the inflexible, irrational, autocratic teacher. Teachers call children cruel names. Teachers assign harsh punishments for "disrespect"— for an "expression on a kid's face," for a kid's trying to use reason in discussing a problem with a teacher, for saying, "But, Mrs. Harshbarker, it wasn't Johnnie's fault. . . ." Teachers assume the stance of "I don't have to put up with . . . anything I don't like." The schools are often run like prisons; the teachers are the omnipotent guards, malicious and sometimes brutal. The children are the prisoners who have no rights, not even human dignity. It is no wonder these kids rebel in the high schools, when they have reached the physical size to defy their teacher-guards who still demand mindless, docile compliance with the teachers' capricious, inhuman treatment. It is also no wonder that vandalism in the United States' schools cost the taxpayers $500 million in 1974 alone. The school, not the home, is the favorite target of vandalism.

The basis of most conflicts between teachers and students is the way teachers interpret the word "discipline." There is no question that discipline is needed in the schools, but there are probably as many different definitions of the word as there are teachers. Unfortunately, too many teachers, especially elementary teachers, approach discipline from an authoritarian stance. It is the authoritarian stance the kids object to and which turns them off, not the discipline. Discipline should be approached from a rational basis, rather than an authoritarian basis. Students want rational rules, fair enforcement of the rules, and appropriate consequences for breaking those rules.

Authoritarianism precludes the necessity to use reason in disciplining students. The authoritarian teacher rules by virtue of his or her position and develops a "Do as I say because I say so" attitude. The teacher assumes no need to be reasonable or use reason in handling the students. After a time, this uncensured power tends to corrupt some teachers and they misuse their positions in high-handed, irrational, dictatorial ways. They no longer use rational judgment at all in handling the students, not even to themselves. Their every whim must be satisfied, no matter how irrational.

Children respond very poorly to this brand of discipline; they consider the teacher unjust and cruel. He probably is. After a time, some of the kids challenge this autocratic omnipotence, either through modeling the teacher's "I don't have to" attitude or through rational defiance of capricious irrationality. Thus, teacher-misbehavior causes child-misbehavior. Teacher-misbehavior will never be questioned if their employers—that's you—don't question it.

But if I interfere, won't they take it out on my kid? They do anyway. The fact that the school has hassled your child is the reason you are reading this.

In fact, the hands-off attitude of parents, brought

about because of fear of retaliation, is the reason that teachers have gotten away with being mini-dictators for years. Fear of retaliation allows the criminal world to operate; it is the same attitude that has allowed inhuman, unproductive classroom management to continue to exist. This fearful parental attitude protects the criminal who runs the classroom and perpetuates the criminal activities in the school.

Many parents don't realize that there are many good teachers who deplore the behavior of their associates and who would like to do something about the mistreatment of children. But their hands are tied because of professional ethics. These good teachers are waiting for someone to untie their hands. They're waiting for help from outside—from parents. Bad teachers will continue their bad practices until the parents protest.

The following pages raise questions concerning some typical teacher-misbehaviors and tell you some things you can do to deal with these problems as well as explaining the theoretical errors that the teachers are making. There *are* procedures to use after first trying and failing to get friendly cooperation from the teacher.

"You lazy, good-for-nothing slob!"

What can I do about a teacher who habitually uses abusive language to Johnnie—when she calls him "fatso," "ugly toad," or "stupid brat"? With an example like this teacher, it is no wonder children misbehave. This teacher, through her miserable modeling, is creating a hostile, threatening environment for the kids. They live in fear (or delight) of the next violent outburst from Ms. Ila Namya. The classroom becomes a place of fear or hilarity, and not much academic learning goes on. The kids view Ms. Namya as either a feared monster or a joke, depending on their sensitivity and on whether they are the recipients or the witnesses to her attacks. The kids remember the names and repeat them, causing hurt feelings and

fights for weeks. With threatened self-concept and threatened psychological safety, children cannot devote much
energy to the business of learning.

Perhaps your goal is a change of teachers for Johnnie, or a change in Ms. Namya's behavior. In either case,
go to the principal and apply Parental Persistence as explained in Chapter 1.

> YOU: I want you to do something about Ms.
> Namya's behavior.

> MR. PRIN CEPAL: I'm sure she didn't mean those
> things. She was probably joking. [He has to say
> this even though he knows better. It's part of pro-
> fessional ethics.]

> YOU: I understand you must say this, but I want
> something done about her name-calling. Johnnie
> has told me that the next time she calls him a name,
> he is going to call her one right back. I've instruct-
> ed him not to do that, but if he is to learn to con-
> trol his behavior, Ms. Namya has to learn to con-
> trol hers.

> MR. CEPAL: That's just her way, Mrs. Parent. The
> kids have all sorts of teachers and must learn to
> take these things in stride. [He's wise to her, but
> he is telling you he cannot or does not want to do
> anything about it. Maybe he needs help.]

> YOU: Johnnie cannot learn when she is constant-
> ly attacking him verbally. I want you to instruct
> her to discontinue her verbal attacks, and I want
> you to do it now.

> MR. CEPAL: [Uncomfortable now. You have put
> him in the position of having to chastise a teacher
> with whom he has to work and from whom he
> wants friendly support.] Well, I'll talk with her,
> but I am not sure that will be the best thing for

Johnnie. [This is the age-old threat of possible retaliation by the teacher. Don't be intimidated into
slinking out of the office.]

YOU: I expect you to control her behavior. If there
is any further abuse of Johnnie, I'll be back to see
you. [You have given him personal motivation for
controlling her and have let him know that you
won't give up.] Now will you talk with her today
so that Johnnie does not have to put up with any
more of her names? [You have set a definite time
and committed him.]

MR. CEPAL: Yes, I'll do what I can. [He is telling
you how weak he is or how strong and impossible
the teacher is.]

YOU: Good, I'll expect no further reports of name-
calling from Johnnie. [You pay his salary to run
the school, and he should be in charge.]

In most cases this will work, but if it does not, you
might have to go back to see him again. If the teacher-
misbehavior continues, go back immediately, and this time
insist that he talk with the teacher in your presence. You
might want to demand that Ms. Namya apologize to Johnnie in your presence. Ms. Namya might deny she called
Johnnie names, or she might resort to tears. Remember that many women use tears of anger as a weapon. If
she lies, insist that other children be called in to support
Johnnie's report. If she cries, tell Mr. Cepal that the tears
are anger tears and are a diversionary tactic to gain his,
and possibly your, sympathy. Ignore the tears and persist
in gaining your end for Johnnie. Apply Parental Persistence until Ms. Ila Namya promises you that she will not
continue her name-calling.

*But what if after all this, she continues in her same
old ways?* She is not likely to continue, but if she does, you
are not whipped yet. You still have a way to go. If the

teacher refuses to willingly learn better behavior, and
her principal is not able to control her, even after several
complaints, then you have to teach both of them that Johnnie has rights and that you, the parents, control the schools
and will have proper behavior from your employees.

TEACH-THE-TEACHER TACTIC

Go into Ms. Namya's classroom in the presence of the
children and call her a "mean, foul-mouthed teacher," and
insist that she apologize to the children for the horrible
names that she has called them. Insist that she explain to
the children that name-calling is wrong and that she
promise to try to control herself in the future. Drastic?
Yes, but it is needed. You are not treating her any worse
than she has been treating the children. She might try to
order you from the room. Don't go. Tell her you are not
leaving until she apologizes and promises to behave better.
If she should attempt to ignore you and continue with her
teaching, enlist the kids. Ask them if they don't think she
should apologize. Conduct a discussion with them about
her behavior. If she does not apologize to them, sooner or
later, she is going to leave the room to get help, probably
from the principal.

When she leaves, keep the kids calm and orderly, and
explain to them that adults sometimes don't always behave
the way they should, and that sometimes they too need
discipline. Explain that you and they will wait quietly until the principal arrives.

When the principal arrives, he will probably come to
you and demand that you leave the classroom. Don't do it.
If he orders you out, quietly tell him you will not leave until the teacher apologizes to the children and promises to
behave. If he attempts to physically remove you, tell him
and others he might enlist to help him to take their hands
off of you, and that he will need a court order to remove you.

Two things could happen at this point. The principal

might decide to remove the children from the room and leave you there. Or he might call the police to arrest you. That is exactly what you want. By bringing in the police, he is opening the problem to the newspapers which delight in reporting school problems. Then you can report the whole episode to the press.

If the children are removed, and you are left alone in the room, you can return for an encore another day. The next time you go, inform the press before you go of what you are doing and that if they want a story, they might want to send a newsperson to accompany you.

The last thing the schools want is bad publicity. If you handle yourself calmly and rationally, you can enlist the press and all the public in putting pressure on the schools to stop some of the miserable treatment of children.

"Suzie's art work indicates she is paranoid-schizophrenic."

How should I respond when Suzie's teacher gives me a "psychological" interpretation of Suzie's art work? Even if Ms. Ipsyche only hints at this sort of thing, reject any consideration of this kind of implication. You do not want to give any credence to this type of diagnosing of Suzie by having a discussion about it. You might as well consult a Ouija board.

> Ms. IPSYCHE: You can see here, Mr. Parent, that in this painting Suzie uses a preponderance of dark colors, deep reds, purples. And here in this drawing she has distorted the human form.
>
> YOU: Yes, I see. It's rather good, isn't it?
>
> Ms. IPSYCHE: Many authorities feel that a choice of predominantly dark colors indicates a depressive personality, and this human distortion indicates that there might be identification and relationship problems, maybe even hostility. [She real-

ly loaded it with "many authorities" to confirm her opinion. And wasn't her choice of words a clever understatement? It is supposed to be "psyche-out Suzie time" now—to discuss all of her foibles. Don't do it.]

YOU: I see a lot of strong, brilliant colors—rather impressive. And the female form reminds me of Henry Moore's sculpture. Maybe Suzie has a talent for art and should be encouraged there. [You spoiled her fun.]

Ms. IPSYCHE: But there are symptoms here that should be considered. [She is calling you obtuse, and she does not want to give up.]

YOU: Where did you get these ideas? Do you also have a degree in psychiatry? [You still aren't playing the game right; you aren't talking about Suzie's problems. And you've probably insulted Ms. Ipsyche.]

Ms. IPSYCHE: No, of course not. But I've done a lot of reading on this, and my experience with children has confirmed many of these things.

YOU: Suzie is a highly imaginative, creative child, and I don't want amateurs psychoanalyzing her. Now, shall we get on with this conference and discuss Suzie's reading skills. I shall be most interested in your opinions about her reading.

Even among the most highly trained people in the psychiatric world, the use of projective techniques, which may be used on children's art work, is controversial. Children's art, which is completely unstructured and nonstandardized, has even less value than the formalized projective "tests" such as the Rorschach, the Draw-a-Man, and the House-Tree-Person tests. Highly trained psychologists and psychiatrists do not agree with each other in interpretation of this kind of material. And certainly no teacher has any business dabbling in this area.

Even if one accepts the theory of projection, the best results that could be obtained from any projective technique would be a projection of a projection, which is to say a blend of the personalities of both the examinee and the examiner. What the examiner perceives of the examinee's perceptions comprises the so-called "objective" results of the test. The result is a blend of the two personalities, one superimposed over the other.

"Pumpkins are not purple!"

What about the teacher who insists that all art work conform to her standards? When you visit your child's classroom, take a good look at the children's art work that is displayed. If many of the drawings look alike, with very little variety represented, beware. At best, that teacher is a rigid personality who is structuring the children's art work to the extent that she is stifling any creativity they might have. Of all places, the art class ought to allow for creativity. If the teacher is programming the children all to do the same thing, she is not allowing for creativity. If a child wants to paint a pumpkin purple, he should be allowed to do so.

If the majority of the children's pictures have a similarity of theme, especially the family portrait, be even more suspicious. This is a clue that the teacher might be practicing psychiatry without a license. Via projective-technique theory, this teacher is forming an opinion of each child's home and family. Test-publishers sell teachers hundreds of little books which explain how to psychoanalyze the child and evaluate the home. This practice is not only a falsely based invasion of privacy, but also it is discriminatory toward children whose family unit is non-standard, children from broken homes and others. These children are made "to feel" their family's difference acutely with art assignments like this.

Teachers have their hands full just teaching the basic skills and trying to be warm human beings to the children. They don't have time to play psychologist, nor the training.

"You mean your parents get drunk and fight, Suzie?"

If Ms. Pry quizzes Suzie about private, family matters, what can I do? This kind of prying can be either conversational questions about the home and parents, or standardized written questions, such as "problem checklists." The written questions might even be an invention of the teacher. Questions on this type of instrument range from such things as, "Do you often bite your fingernails?" to "Do your mother and father fight often?" Other questions include such things as, "Do you often have nightmares?" "Do you have a brother or sister of whom you are jealous?" "Do your parents like you?" and "Is money a problem in your home?"

Some school systems have long had policies which require a parent's signature before any psychological tests can be given to a child, but not all do. A new wave of rights to privacy and children's rights has brought about some new state and federal laws governing this sort of school snooping. But parents should know that unofficial prying goes on in some classrooms, and the results are not filed in the official records which are subject to scrutiny and challenging.

No parent should ever sign documents which give a school system permission to give tests of this type which are commonly known as personality tests, problem checklists, surveys, or any other euphemism the schools can dream up to conceal from the parents what they are really doing.

Personality tests of any type are controversial among

the best-trained people in the psychology profession, whether the tests are question-and-answer "checklists" or projective techniques. Research done on the best of these tests reveals virtually no validity or reliability. So even in the hands of the highly skilled psychologist, these tests are highly suspect.

Certainly no schoolperson has any business using these instruments, neither the counselor nor school psychologist—least of all the classroom teacher. Counselors and school psychologists have had very little training, if any, in the use of these particular tests, and if their training were adequate, they probably would not use them.

The classroom teacher has had no training for using this kind of instrument and has no business using it. Ironically, it seems that the people who know the least about devices of this type are the very people who do use them and consequently do injustice to your child. This subject is discussed at greater length in the chapter entitled "Parent's Guide to School Records and Test Scores."

What can I do about this? Prevention is the best approach to this problem. When you enroll your child in any new school, present written instructions to the school that your child is not to be given any psychological or sociological tests, checklists or surveys without your written permission. This way, you guard against so-called "psychological diagnosis" of your child, after which it is often too late to do anything about it. Once a label is put on your child by the school, there is nothing you can do to take it out of the minds of the school personnel, even if you do get the written evidence expunged from the records.

Another example of the drug-store psychology employed by teachers known to few parents is the *observation* checklists teachers fill out on your child unbeknown to child or parents. These checklists are variously entitled such as "Behavior Checklists," or "Checklists for Disturbed Behaviors." As you read a reproduction of one actually used in Chapter VI, you will see that all normal children exhibit most of these behaviors at various times. These "goodies" are recommended to teachers at many teacher-training institutions. You should keep in mind that most of the teachers encouraged to use these "objective" observation devices have had no more preparation than one or two basic survey courses in psychology and educational psychology.

If you were not able to prevent this kind of invasion of privacy, apply Parental Persistence in the presence of the principal to retrieve all written observation reports. This expunging of records will not expunge the minds of the educators, but it will put on record your refusal to accept this type of diagnosis of Suzie.

TEACH-THE-TEACHER TACTIC

If you wish, you could preface your Parental Persistence demand with an object lesson with both the teacher and the principal. Take a list of questions with you and solicitously ask them such things as: "How old are you?" "What is your IQ?" "Why are/aren't you married?" "How is your sex life?" "Do you practice birth control?" "Does your husband/friend/wife have affairs with others?" Treat the questions seriously—if you are the kind of person who could pull this off. When they begin sputtering, tell them with a serious demeanor that if they do not answer, that you will have to fill out the form as best you can from your observations of the way they are now behaving, or that you will have to go to other sources to get this much needed information in order to decide whether or not they are suitable people to be employed to work with children. When they tell you that these things are none of your business, agree with them and then inform them that the things they have been asking Suzie are none of their business. Then begin to apply Parental Persistence to stop the school's invasion of privacy.

"Spankings, Shakings, Slaps, and Slugs"

If a teacher, a vice-principal or "advisor" slaps, hits, or "kicks around" my child, what can I do? Friendly cooperation is obviously a waste of time with a person who habitually beats children. The use of Parental Persistence in conference with the offender's principal with threat of lawsuit will probably be a pretty good bet for keeping the bully's hands off your child. Parents in a number of states have filed lawsuits against teachers for physical violence to children. More lawsuits of this type would greatly decrease child-beating.

Laws against corporal punishment protect every group in our society except children. Beating of wives, flogging of sailors, physical punishment of institutionalized criminals and mental patients all have been banned. Even the beating of animals is illegal. Only children have no protection against physical abuse. Hitting an adult is considered assault, but hitting a child is considered discipline.

No parent has to allow his child to be a punching bag for ill-tempered, educator-bullies. While it is true that most of the public schools in the United States permit physical punishment, don't let the school bully you with this British tradition. Corporal punishment is illegal in most of the countries in the world, except for the United States and other English-speaking countries. But some states have laws against corporal punishment.

Even in states in which corporal punishment is legal, use of physical punishment is a precarious prerogative which no parent should allow. The schools know that whenever they use physical punishment, they open themselves to lawsuit and highly negative publicity. States which legally permit corporal punishment regulate use of it so restrictively that schools do not *legally* invoke the "right" very often. The "spanking" must be done in the presence of impartial witnesses, often including the parents and with their permission, to prove that there was no malice and no excessive abuse. If parents were to force schools to observe every article of the laws, there would be no corporal punishment in the schools of any state.

Probably ninety-nine percent of physical punishment of schoolchildren does not comply with the law. Most spankings, shakings, slaps and slugs result from teachers' temper-tantrums.

Never sign a consent-form which allows a school to punish your child physically; this form is the school's legal protection from you. Don't sign away your rights. In fact, we suggest that you put in writing an instrument which has the opposite effect, a statement which specifically denies the school permission to use physical punishment on your child. The only child who would respond positively to appropriately dispense corporal punishment is a child whose parents have used physical punishment to the exclusion of all other types of discipline in training that child.

Any educator who uses physical punishment to control children's behavior has identified himself as a person whose mentality is not adequate to deal with children. If he must use physical punishment, he has given up the best tool an educator is supposed to have—his superior knowledge of child behavior. If an educator does not possess adequate tools for dealing with children short of physical abuse, that educator has no place in the schools. Most of the misfits who use physical punishment are inadequate in many ways, often people of small intellect and/or inadequate personality development, who must repeatedly disprove their own sense of inadequacy by beating on children.

TEACH-THE-TEACHER TACTIC

If you have expressed a complaint to the building principal concerning physical mistreatment of your child, but the building principal is apparently not able to control his teachers' behavior, you must protect your child. If another incident of physical violence occurs after you have registered your objections with the principal, then Mark Desade has proven that either he has no intention of controlling his behavior or that he cannot control his own behavior. You must act.

Go to the local police station which serves the school your child attends and file a police report. This is a simple procedure that will take about twenty minutes of your time.

When the duty officer talks with you, simply explain the situation. Explain to the police that you have requested cooperation from the school, but that the school has chosen to ignore your requests. Tell the police that you want an official police report on record concerning the matter, and that you do not wish to press charges at this time. Signing a complaint of assault and battery is a more drastic action you can take later if needed. Save that option for another time if it is needed. Remember, your goal is to stop the teacher's abusive behavior, not to make a "federal case" of the matter. Explain that position to the police so that they understand your intentions; the police will appreciate your parental concern and respond positively to a rational, calmly stated wish to stop violent behavior.

After talking with you, a policeman will visit the teacher concerned and talk with him to get his side of the story. That is exactly what you want. No doubt, Mark Desade will lie profusely to the police to protect himself, denying any abusive behavior. That is to be expected, but you will have accomplished your goal. Mark Desade is on notice that you will not continue to tolerate physical abuse, and you will go outside the school channels for protection of your child. This police report will become a permanent record of a teacher's violent behavior, and that report might protect your child in the long run.

Mark Desade will be angry with you for doing this,

but he was abusively angry evidently before you resorted to this tactic. At least, you will protect your child from any further physical abuse. You will also be cooling off a situation which could erupt into a very bad scene for your child. If an abusive teacher continues to abuse a child, sooner or later that child is going to erupt and strike back. You can be very sure that as soon as that happens, even to the slightest degree, the child will be thrown out of school at least, and possibly have assault charges filed against him if he is an older student. Most of the increasing number of assaults on teachers are provoked by increasingly abusive teacher behavior.

Under no circumstances should a parent let himself be provoked into physical retaliation against any school personnel. If a parent so much as touches one of the bullies, he will find himself slapped with an assault charge and some highly derogatory newspaper publicity. News items of this type are increasing in small, local newspapers. The schools do not hesitate to file police charges. Children should have the same protection.

"You're a liar, Suzie!"

If Suzie comes home from school upset because the teacher unjustly accused her of lying or cheating, what can I do to remedy the situation? This is a difficult problem that many parents have experienced and have not known how to handle with their children, let alone the teacher. Most parents weakly tell their child that "sometimes this happens, and that it is part of living—to be accused of doing something one hasn't done." This feeble explanation is not very effective to the child and does not ever repair the rupture of the teacher-pupil relationship.

What Suzie needs at this point is an apology from Ms. Ura Lyre, to restore her faith in the teacher's fairness. You should be able to effect such an apology by applying Parental Persistence in the presence of the principal:

YOU: Ms. Lyre, you have falsely accused Suzie of lying, you have destroyed all of Suzie's confidence in you as a fair person, and this is interfering with your ability to teach her. To correct this, I want you to apologize to Suzie to show her that you are human, and that sometimes teachers make mistakes too. [You've thought this through and know exactly what you want before you go into conference.]

MS. LYRE: Why, I didn't really accuse her of lying. I'm sure she must have misunderstood me. She is taking this much too seriously. [Ms. Lyre is now lying to you, but it can be expected as a typical response. Don't argue the point with her.]

YOU: Good, then you won't mind explaining this to Suzie. I want this cleared up right now because Suzie does think it is serious. Let's call Suzie in and clear up the misunderstanding. [You didn't tumble to being placated so that you would leave and have to do the clean-up job with Suzie.]

MS. LYRE: [Uncomfortable now.] Mrs. Parent, I think you are making too much of this. It wasn't anything. [She is belittling your concern; you're supposed to feel like a fool. Don't. Ms. Lyre doesn't want to admit her error.]

YOU: It is important to Suzie's sense of fairness and honesty, and I want you to correct the error. [You have stuck to your guns, and you are forcing Ms. Lyre to support her disclaimer to you where it counts—to Suzie.]

MR. PRINCE EPAL: Probably, Ms. Lyre, we can clear this up quickly if we do what Mrs. Parent wants. [He wants to end the thing as easily and quickly as possible. He has ordered Ms. Lyre to back down since you evidently won't be put off by their pooh-poohing the incident.]

Ms. Lyre: [Grudgingly.] Well, all right, but I consider it completely unnecessary.

A favorite tactic of educators is to pooh-pooh children's responses and parental complaints of teacher-misbehavior. This is their way of shaming parents for insisting that teachers be responsible for their behavior. Probably Ms. Lyre's accusation was not important in her mind, but a thoughtless or careless remark to a child can sometimes do great damage. This is a form of tyranny that adults can exercise over children, and that we cannot afford to allow in those to whom we entrust our young children.

If the problem had centered about the teacher's accusing the child of cheating on academic work, the same procedure could be used to request that the teacher restructure the task to check on the child's knowledge of the material. A retesting would decide objectively whether or not the child knows the material, which is the issue. An accusation of cheating is never in order from a teacher and does not do anyone any good. If a child has cheated, a retesting would teach the child what he should know about cheating, and the teacher will not have created any ill-will with the child. A simple retesting also checks out the teacher's perceptions of what was observed as "cheating."

Teach-the-Teacher Tactic

Go to the teacher with a fabricated story about some horrible thing she has done in class (not her accusation of Suzie). Accuse the teacher of those acts and watch her deny them. When Ms. Lyre is finished with her indignant denial, explain that she might now understand how Suzie felt when she was unjustly accused of lying. Then you could say, "I'll apologize to you after you apologize to Suzie." If the teacher is a sharpie and has a good sense of

humor, she'll forgive you, but don't bank on it. The sharp-
ies are not the ones who attack kids with false accusations.

"Dear Parent, Johnnie was a bad boy again today..."

*If a teacher makes it a practice to send notes home com-
plaining about Johnnie's behavior, what should I do?* The
first thing not to do is to raise hell with Johnnie. If the
teacher is not performing her job at school, there is no
reason Mom and Dad should pick up the teacher's chips
and clean house on Johnnie. There needs to be cooperation,
but the school has to carry its burden. Ms. Itell is passing
the buck and giving you the task of being unpleasant, and
handling her job for her.

One approach to the problem is simply to ignore the
notes, not rewarding the teacher for sending them and
therefore reducing or extinguishing this behavior. But
that approach is not in keeping with the philosophy that
parents should be actively involved.

You might have to observe Ms. Itell's classroom to
determine in what areas she is failing, so that you can tell
her what she is doing wrong and how she can handle her
job. Look for alternate methods for handling Johnnie to
suggest to Ms. Itell. For example, if you observe that Ms.
Itell stresses negative marks and comments on papers and
in conversation with the children, convey your thought
to her:

> YOU: You know, Ms. Itell, we have found that
> Johnnie responds much better to positive sugges-
> tions from us than he does to negative criticism. It
> works with him.

> MS. ITELL: Why, I am always positive with the
> children.

> YOU: I'm sure you try, but Johnnie responds very
> favorably to positive suggestion, and he needs lots
> of encouragement; we all do.

Ms. ITELL: Well ... I do the best I can. [A negative approach in itself.]

YOU: I know you work very hard, but I want you to try more positive encouragement with Johnnie. I think you'll be surprised at how well it works. Will you give it a try?

Ms. ITELL: [Skeptical] Of course, but ... [If she is a conscientious teacher who is really trying, she'll give it some thought and work on it.]

If Ms. Itell attempts to unload on you about all of Johnnie's misbehavior, don't encourage her, but if she unloads anyway, the worst thing you can do is to agree with her about how terrible Johnnie is. Be positive about Johnnie and suggest that she consider some of Johnnie's good traits and teach to his strengths. Nobody is all bad, not even Johnnie—if the teacher can only allow herself to think of him positively. Tell her how good Johnnie is at home and how many things he can do at home. Even if you are having some minor problems with Johnnie, be careful about telling her too much. Ms. Itell is looking for support for her negative feelings about Johnnie. Don't you be the one to give the teacher the ammunition to use against him.

If Ms. Itell can mentally relegate Johnnie to the "bad kid" classification at school and at home, you are going to help her establish in Johnny a negative self-fulfilling prophecy. This means that if Johnnie is treated as a bad kid at school, he is going to become a bad kid because he doesn't really have any other choice. He is being programmed to be a bad kid.

Ms. ITELL: Mrs. Parent, I am really at my wit's end. Johnnie is creating such a ruckus that the rest of us cannot get anything done.

YOU: What is it specifically that Johnnie does

that keeps the rest of you from working? [Force her to deal in specific behaviors, not her feelings.]

MS. ITELL: All kinds of things. [She has generalized it so much that she does not cope with specific behaviors which is a common teacher error.]

YOU: [Encouragingly.] Give me an example.

MS. ITELL: Well, yesterday when another student, a lovely model child, mispronounced a word, Johnnie let out a loud, raucous laugh that completely stopped the class and caused all the other children to laugh. It took me five minutes to regain control.

YOU: Do the other children laugh at Johnnie when he makes mistakes?

MS. ITELL: Yesss ... sometimes, I suppose, but not like that.

YOU: What does this particular incident tell you about Johnnie, aside from the fact that he annoys you and disturbs your class?

MS. ITELL: A need to be cruel, I guess.

YOU: That's negative, Ms. Itell. Try thinking of it from Johnnie's point of view. It was improper behavior, but why did he need to laugh at the girl?

MS. ITELL: Well, if you mean retaliation, that is not an excuse . . .

YOU: No, I don't mean retaliation. That, again, is a negative view of Johnnie. Do you see what I am getting at? What does Johnnie need that might keep him from laughing at others' mistakes?

MS. ITELL: I suppose if the other children didn't laugh at his mistakes. [Good, you're getting her there.]

YOU: And how could you be of help there?

Ms. ITELL: I suppose if his phonics were better, he would mispronounce fewer words.

YOU: Good. Now you know one positive way to help Johnnie and at the same time handle your problem with him in the classroom. Now can you think of one personality trait of Johnnie's that you like?

Ms. ITELL: Certainly. He has a very sunny disposition, and even when I scold him he doesn't get angry or sulky.

YOU: Do you suppose you could figure out some ways that you can capitalize on that?

Ms. ITELL: I really don't know.

YOU: Will you think about it?

Ms. ITELL: Of course, but ... [She's having trouble with her negative attitude toward Johnnie, but there is a chance she can learn.]

YOU: Good. I'm glad we could have this little talk today, and I think if you will work on some positive attitudes toward Johnnie, your problems with him will decrease. I'll check back with you in a couple of weeks to see how things are going. [This way, you are "putting her on" to work on positive attitudes so that she cannot just forget this discussion.]

If you haven't time to go to school again, write the teacher a note about how good Johnnie is at home and/or demand for the next day a list of ten to twenty things Johnnie does right to illustrate her "positive" approach to Johnnie.

Some friends of ours handled this situation differently. They kept getting notes from the teacher which were very poorly written. The parents corrected the misspelled

words, the grammar, the punctuation, and sent the note
back to the teacher with a grade on the note. They received no further notes.

"Your mother told me ..."

*When I confide something about Suzie to the teacher who
betrays this confidence to Suzie, how should I react?* This
is a relatively minor problem on the surface, but it is a
clue to a fear of parental communication on the part of
the teacher, and perhaps on the part of the system. By be-
traying parent confidences or criticizing parents to a
child, and generally embarrassing the child, the teacher
is pressuring the child to keep his parents away from the
school. This tactic bespeaks a "parents-keep-out" attitude.
If the school is fearful of parents, then the school is hiding
something, probably the mishandling of children.

Your primary concern is your child and your relationship to your child. Until you know a teacher through experience to be a warm, secure human being, do not confide in her. Confidences about a child might very well be
used by an insecure teacher against the child in an effort
to control both you and the child. Start from that stance,
and you can always alter it after you know the teacher
is trustworthy.

If you have fallen into this trap inadvertently or
through your own basic trust, you must repair your relationship with your child, and you should feel no obligation to protect Ms. Bee Tray in mending your far more
important relationship with your child. It is always good
when you can support the teacher and the school to your
child, but when it comes to a choice between the two, your
relationship with your child takes precedence. Even if it
means destroying the teacher's credibility, that is what
you must do. The teacher's relationship with the child will
be of short duration, whereas yours is long-term and
critically important. If Ms. Bee Tray, for self-serving rea-

sons, does not work to build your child's self-image as she develops his basic skills, then you owe her nothing.

> SUZIE: Mom, Ms. Tray said that you told her that you have "one heck of a time" getting me to study my spelling words, that I am a "dawdler." Why did you have to tell her that? It's so embarrassing.
>
> YOU: Yes, I suppose I did say that, honey, and I was wrong and I'm sorry I told her that. It's no fun to be embarrassed.
>
> SUZIE: Oh, it's ok, it's not that important, but I wish Ms. Tray hadn't said it in front of all those other kids, just because I was fooling around when I should have been doing my arithmetic. [Now you see how Ms. Tray used you against your child. Ms. Tray needn't have brought you into her correction of Suzie's behavior. Maybe it was a slip, but again, maybe it was intentional. Either way, it was poor judgment and does not build a positive relationship between home and school.]
>
> YOU: Ms. Tray was wrong in saying that to you, Suzie, especially in front of the other kids, but I promise you that I won't tell her anything else she might use that way. OK?
>
> SUZIE: OK, Mom.

Obviously, Ms. Bee Tray does not wish to encourage a cooperative relationship with the home, and she does not deserve further confidences.

"Everything that goes on here, stays here."

What if Johnnie tells me that the teacher instructed him not to discuss school problems at home? The best kind of public relations a school can obtain is the kids themselves —or the worst kind. When a teacher is defensively guarded, she herself is aware of teacher-conduct to which parents would object. This kind of wall between school and home is poor public relations, and this kind of interference between parent and child is unhealthy, violating every tenet of child-rearing.

As in the answer to the previous question, repair your right to communication with your child. Instruct Johnnie that he should discuss with you anything that he wishes. Tell him that you are not only responsible for raising him, but also you are responsible for the proper running of the school. Explain to Johnnie that the teacher was wrong to say that, and that the school has no right to try to gag communication between children and their parents.

Then, start visiting the school frequently to find out more about what is going on there. And definitely discuss the school with Johnnie to learn more about what goes on when visitors are not present. Public-relations newsletters to parents from the superintendent's office may proclaim a school system "beautiful," but what the kids say about school is more truthful and reliable information.

"I'm afraid, Mommie."

What is wrong if Johnnie refuses to go to school? If young Johnnie consistently doesn't want to go to school, there is something going on there that shouldn't be going on. Don't attribute this attitude to some insufficiency on the part of the child. Most children welcome new experiences, including school, and they enjoy new experiences unless something goes afoul with the new experience. A child who doesn't want to go to school probably feels threatened in some way at school.

Find out what the reason is. The young child may not be able to give you a reason because he might not understand it himself. He might understand only that the place is unpleasant. It may be the teacher's attitude toward him or it may be the attitude of the other children. If it is the latter, then the teacher is not properly managing the class, or he is modeling poorly; that is, he is reflecting bad attitudes toward your child that the other children are imitating.

Take Johnnie by the hand and go to school with him and say, "We'll find out what the trouble is." Do *not* talk with the teacher. Simply make this a visitation day during which you sit and observe in order to determine what the problem is. If there is not a specific incident Johnnie can relate to you, then there is a generalized problem that you are going to be better able to pick up than the teacher is. You might have to visit the classroom several days in order to figure out what the problem is, but figure it out for yourself. And *then* tackle the teacher.

Don't tell the teacher that Johnnie doesn't want to come to school, that he is afraid; don't give him that handle. You don't know his motives, and you might be playing right into his hands by revealing that his possible misbehavior is working. After you have determined the cause of the fear, then apply Parental Persistence to correct the problem.

There are teachers who control students through fear, and they are pleased if a child is afraid of them—as long as the child obeys. When a child is frightened, the only solution is a change of teachers. A young child cannot learn from a teacher of whom he is afraid.

"Write a thousand-word paper on 'I must respect the teacher.'"

What can I do if the teacher gives academic work as punishment? The teacher who does this is teaching the kids that academic work is punishment. This, of course, is educationally and psychologically unsound. If a teacher, or anyone, wants a child to learn that a particular activity is something to be enjoyed, giving that activity as punishment is the best way to destroy enjoyment of that activity.

The teacher who employs this tactic is working

against herself; when she sometimes uses academic activity as punishment, more of the kids will resist regular academic assignments, because they have associated that activity with punishment, something undesirable. Then the teacher will have to try to force the kids to do their assignments; she will have to stand over them with a "big stick," and she doesn't have very many big sticks to use on them. Grudging compliance on the part of the students will not produce academic accomplishment.

Typical academic punishments include: Doing fifty extra math problems, writing a ten-page theme, or writing "I will not laugh at the teacher," a hundred times. At best, the child will turn in a sloppy performance since he knows it is the punishment that counts, not the quality.

Parental Persistence should be used to request that Ms. Worksbad not give Suzie this type of punishment:

> YOU: Ms. Worksbad, I understand that all teachers have some behavior problems with which they must cope, but I want Suzie to learn to like math (or writing, or whatever), and I don't want you to use math as a punisher for her.

> MS. WORKSBAD: Well, I have to use something to control them, and that little assignment won't hurt her. In fact, it will be good for her. She could use a little extra work on math anyway.

> YOU: I'm sure she can use some extra work on her math, but to present it as a punishment is the best way to "turn her off" to math, and I don't want you to use math or any academic work as punishment. Do you suppose you could find or design some interesting extra math activities for Suzie that could be presented as an exciting, desirable activity, not a punishment?

> MS. WORKSBAD: [Indignant.] Of course I could.

You: Excellent, then I want you to do just that, and refrain from using math problems as a punishment. Will you do that?

Ms. Worksbad: That's going to be a lot of work, but I'll see what I can do.

Teach-the-Teacher Tactic

You might apply Parental Persistence with her in the presence of her principal by asking her for a written report of her rationale for assigning academic work as punishment. Insist that she document her philosophy with educational and psychological theory for justifying this type of assignment. The teacher will probably back down before you have to really *insist* that she complete this academic punishment task. Either she will back down or her principal will insist that she back down, because it has been known for scores of years that academic punishment is unsound—even though some teachers still persist in using it.

"Perhaps you should punish him, Mrs. Parent."

What about the teacher request that I take away Johnnie's privileges at home because he isn't doing his schoolwork? No teacher is going to ask you to add privileges at home for what Johnnie does do at school; therefore, she has no business requesting that you use punishment at home. The teacher is trying to get you on her side against your child.

If you treat Johnnie as though he were a "bad" kid at home, and the teacher treats him as a "bad" kid at school, then he becomes convinced that he is a "bad" kid. It is psychologically unhealthy and is the kind of thing that leads to juvenile delinquency. A child treated this way has no refuge, no place he feels safe, which everyone needs.

The teacher that makes this request of parents is

asking them to pick up his chips for him. If his ways of managing his classroom are not working, then he should find some other ways of handling his job. If he cannot, then he should get out of the classroom.

Probably this teacher is using only negative methods for handling Johnnie at school since he suggests this form of handling him to you. He is giving you insight into his educational philosophy. Perhaps he should learn some positive ways to handle Johnnie at school, which would solve the problem. He might devise some privileges Johnnie could earn by doing what teacher wants him to do. If Johnnie is an older child, the teacher might revise his own attitude toward Johnnie by looking for some good things about him or his performance.

"All children cheat and lie."

What about the teacher who says or implies that all children cheat and lie? If this is Ms. Hatte Kid's assumption, then you may be sure that she cheats and lies and that she is making this assumption based on her own lack of moral standards. This teacher is dangerous; she will create conditions in her classroom which will reward lying and cheating by the children in her classroom. She encourages lying and cheating by assuming they all do it, by expecting this type of behavior, she'll produce it. A person who makes this assumption about children really doesn't have much faith in children (or people, in general), or in their potential. Nor does she have any faith in her role as leader. Ms. Hatte Kid should not be working with children. But you, the parent, are forewarned in that you have gained knowledge about this teacher's orientation if any other problems with her arise.

"That's not my job!"

And what if this teacher does not consider the promotion of honesty and fairness among the children as part of her job? This teacher is lacking some very basic information about her job. Lying and cheating are components of a value system. Value systems are taught not only in the home, but also in the school where children spend a good percentage of their waking hours. Teachers have a responsibility to teach "high moral values," and the teacher who assumes all children are dishonest has denied this aspect of her job.

Honesty and fairness are learned within the peer-group. The home does not have twenty-five or thirty kids in it among whom parents can teach these interpersonal values. While it is true that the home is responsible for moral values, the practice of universals such as honesty and truth must extend to the school which provides the setting in which the children can experience and practice these values beyond the family group in the child's extended world. If parents don't insist that the teachers teach honesty and fairness, the teachers are probably not going to do it. Of course, the teaching of these values assumes a fair and honest teacher.

The teacher who says she is not responsible for teaching moral values is teaching values nevertheless; she is teaching that there are no moral values. If the children do not experience a moral value-system working, then they cannot know what it is, except as empty words. By default, that teacher is teaching that "anything goes," and that getting caught is the only "wrong." Although religion legally does not have a place in the public schools, and has been pushed further and further out of the public schools in recent years, this is no excuse for the schools abandoning all moral values. Unfortunately, many teachers equate moral values with religion and do not insist upon even the values of honesty and fairness.

The abandonment of moral values in the classrooms in recent years is probably one of the worst influences on our total society. And it is very likely to get worse in years to come unless the parents of children do something about it. A lack of moral values creates a great many of the school problems with which the teachers and students struggle.

This problem could be handled through reform of board objectives and personnel policies of the school system, and this would take group parental action. This is a generalized problem that cannot be handled on an individual basis except inasmuch as you are the defender through Parental Persistence of your own child's basic integrity.

"Adults always tell the truth, and children always lie."

If Johnnie reports frequent teacher-misbehavior and the teacher denies all of it, what can I do? By denying all of it, the teacher has labeled Johnnie a liar, a fabricator of wild tales. This is one of the most common practices within the teaching profession. Not only do bad teachers commit *unjust* acts against children, but when they are reported for doing it, they declare that the child is a liar. How many times have you heard of a teacher admitting to mishandling a child? How often do you hear of a teacher apologizing to a child for her misconduct? Yet, we all know that all of us occasionally lose our tempers, say things we shouldn't, and mishandle a situation. Most people admit mistakes and sometimes apologize for them. Why is it that teachers never make mistakes—to hear them tell it?

A child is fair game, not only for the mistreatment, but also for the liar-label if he reports the incident. The helpless child is in a "no-win" position because he *is* a child. It is assumed that adults are more honest than children. This, of course, is not true. Most children are far more honest than most adults. Even if a child attempts to be dishonest, he hasn't the artifice or the sophistication to carry it off. A child's fib is generally recognizable, and it is generally easier to get the truth from a child than it is from an adult.

The adult who lies generally has a very good reason for doing it. The teacher who lies to cover her misconduct is protecting her job and her career, and those are very "heavy" items, especially in a surplus-teacher market. The teacher who lies thinks she cannot afford to admit a mistake; this type of person is a threatened person. Threatened teachers are often guilty of misconduct.

You know your child. You know what he is capable of doing and what he is not capable of doing. You know what charges against him are plausible and which are not plausible. You know your child's capacity for fibbing, and you generally know when he is doing so. If you have a good relationship with your child, you can almost always get the truth from him. It is only the very rare young child who successfully lies to parents who want the truth.

You generally do not know the adult teacher with whom you might be dealing, but you do know that the teacher very likely has high motivation for not admitting to mistakes. When a teacher says one thing and the child another, believe your child. The standard practice of always taking the teacher's word occurs so frequently in some schools that that school is teaching the children about the rewards for lying.

By ostensibly accepting a teacher's lies instead of your child's truth, even though you know better, you are doing your child a great disservice. You are then allowing the school to use you against your own child, and you are teaching your child that lying pays off. If you placate a dishonest teacher in an effort to preserve the peace, don't be too surprised if your child does begin to lie to you. If you want to raise an honest child, don't allow him to suffer at the hands of dishonesty—when you *can* help it. The least you can do is label the teacher for what she is and let your child know that you believe in him and are on his side against injustice.

If Johnnie comes home from school irate that a teacher has lied to protect herself, talk with the principal, set the record straight, and label the teacher for what she is, if there is no way to corroborate Johnnie's story. If enough parents were to do this, eventually that teacher could not continue to successfully protect herself with the "your word against mine" tactic.

"I have thirty other students."

What can I do when Ms. Poorme pleads she hasn't time to devote to Johnnie's needs because she has thirty other students to consider? One way or another Ms. Poorme is going to be bothered by Johnnie's problems, and if she doesn't take care of them in a positive manner, she is going to end up using a lot of punishment. She is in essence saying to you that she will not consider any method of handling Johnnie except using excessive punishment. Punishment is probably her approach to handling all thirty of the children in her room. She is revealing that she thinks of the children not as individuals but as a group. They do not exist for her as individual human beings.

By saying she has no time for Johnnie, Ms. Poorme is saying that she does not have any respect for him. If she is allowed to practice this attitude, Johnnie will return her attitude by losing respect for his teacher. Johnnie's behavior under these circumstances can do nothing but deteriorate.

If a teacher makes this statement to you, a change of teacher is in order. She has quit her job as far as your Johnnie is concerned. Quote her statement and use Parental Persistence to obtain a change of teacher for Johnnie.

"Suzie demands too much attention."

If Ms. Dona Gottime implies or states that Suzie seeks attention, demanding too much of the teacher's time because of parental indulgence or parental neglect, what can be done to correct this impression? Granted that no teacher can give any child the kind of attention that the child might be given at home, each child is entitled to some attention from the teacher. A curious child can be a big nuisance to a harried teacher. Unfortunately, some teachers solve their own problems by declaring the oversimplification that Suzie demands too much attention when in actuality it is the teacher's inability to handle all the children's needs.

Because Ms. Gottime acts on this opinion by attempting to extinguish Suzie's requests for help, the teacher gets the kid off her back, but Suzie is taught only that her curiosity and attempts to get help are improper behavior. Soon, Suzie resigns herself to lethargic acceptance of this unstimulating situation. Suzie's learning slows down to a monotonous grind; school is a bore. All spontaneity and intellectual curiosity have been snuffed out. Suzie is now "socialized" as the teacher wants her to be. The teacher's inadequacy problem is solved. The American school has triumphed once more.

Teachers can be far off base in their estimation of the cause of a .child's demand on. their time. Teachers' time-allotment problems are too often resolved by attaching a psychoanalytic label of "attention-seeking" to children who challenge a teacher's efficiency and/or intelligence. Should you suspect this attitude toward your Suzie, you should correct Ms. Dona Gottime's faulty judgment immediately. If you don't correct this teacher error, the teacher's method of handling Suzie could be wrong for Suzie.

> Ms. DONA GOTTIME: Mrs. Parent, Suzie is entirely too dependent on adults. I'm beginning a program now to help her to be more self-sufficient. [Isn't it amazing how the teacher's efficiency problems become psychological diagnoses of the children! She is actually saying, "I'm trying to get that kid off my back, but I'll couch it in psychological judgment of Suzie to confound the parent and get parent cooperation."]

YOU: That is quite a judgment of Suzie. What is it that Suzie does that causes you to say that about her? [Make her deal in specifics.]

MS. GOTTIME: Well, she's always asking questions, questions about things that are completely off the subject. Yesterday when we were talking about Indian clothing, she interrupted with a question about how the pilgrims talked with the Indians, what language they used.

YOU: Did you answer her, or had you started your new program?

MS. GOTTIME: Since it was irrelevant, I ignored the question. She has to learn to control herself and not dominate every discussion. [Did the teacher ignore Suzie because the question interfered with the teacher's plan for the day, or was the teacher stumped for an answer to the question?]

YOU: I don't think that question was irrelevant. It showed that Suzie's mind was truly involved in the subject. You should have simply answered the question with a quick answer or said, "I don't know" if you didn't and then gone on with your planned discussion of Indian clothing. A curious mind deals with many aspects of any subject, not just what is under specific consideration.

MS. GOTTIME: But she does this kind of thing too much. It's not fair to the other children. [She really means, it is not fair to the teacher.] She is improving now though since I've stopped answering all of her questions.

YOU: I'm sorry to hear that, because we've always encouraged her to be curious and ask questions. I want you to answer her questions when you can. Asking questions is one of the best ways for children to learn. It is your job to encourage questioning and to help children find appropriate sources of information for answering questions.

MS. GOTTIME: It's always a problem for teachers when children have been overindulged at home. [Gotcha! She's taken a swack at you, accusing you of ruining your child. It is anger. Don't return it.]

YOU: I'm sure it is a problem to deal with the many needs of many children which good teachers do; but Suzie is a very responsible, obedient child, and we've encouraged her intellectual curiosity, yes. We don't call that overindulgence. If we don't know the answer, we suggest she keep the question in mind until we can look up the answer together. Would you try using this procedure with her? I think it would work beautifully.

MS. GOTTIME: [Reluctantly] Oh, I suppose I can try it. [She doesn't appear convinced, but you've vetoed her psychological disposal of Suzie. And you just might have planted an idea in the teacher's mind that might grow to make her a better teacher.]

"I, Johnnie, promise not to spit and bite."

What about the teacher who prides herself on her behavior-modification techniques and has Johnnie sign contracts to refrain from behaving in ways in which he doesn't behave anyway? This teacher has an excellent system going for suggesting all sorts of "wonderful" behaviors to Johnnie. She is suggesting ways in which he can defend himself from her mishandling. By signing the contract, Johnnie admits that he is normally guilty of this kind of behavior; the child is trapped—damned if he does sign it and damned if he does not sign it.

It is a good idea to instruct your child never to sign

anything without your presence. A contract is a business instrument, and it is unfair for a child to have to deal with an adult in a business relationship. Contracts between adults and minors are illegal because adults are known to take advantage of children. If anything is important enough to draw up a written contract, the parents should be party to it. This way, you'll have adults dealing with adults. But then, only the child will sign with the teacher; don't you sign anything even if you should permit your child to sign.

You might work up a "contract" for the teacher to sign. It might read: "If I, Ms. Connie Track, refrain from calling Johnnie names, refrain from losing my patience and temper, and if I treat Johnnie as a human being for ten days, Johnnie will stay away from school for one day to make my job easier for me." Of course, she won't sign it, but she'll get the message. You will be using behavior modification on her.

"Go to the office! Get out!"

When a teacher constantly sends Johnnie to the principal's office, what can be done? Find out the teacher's reasons for sending Johnnie to the principal so frequently. Talk with the teacher and tell her that you are willing to work with her to develop alternative methods of handling the situation. You must teach her to explore alternatives to this defeating teacher behavior, defeating for her and certainly defeating for Johnnie. When he is sent to the office, Johnnie cannot make amends for his misconduct, and he is wasting valuable study time on his trip to the office and during the time spent there, time which might better be spent learning and practicing correct behavior if he were given the chance. The whole act is negative, from a learning standpoint and from the student's attitudinal and emotional standpoint. It is a teacher cop-out. She is saying, "I can't handle it."

If Ms. Cana Handle does not respond to your positive

suggestions that you jointly plan alternative measures, she is behaving worse than her pupils by clinging to her inadequate, defeating behavior. She admits defeat every time she sends a pupil from her classroom. By using only one negative correction device, she is making the same error as the teacher who keeps kids in from recess for all infractions.

In this case, you will probably have to apply Parental Persistence concerning alternative measures in a conference you arrange in the presence of the teacher's administrator. This way, the teacher's behavior is recorded as objectionable, and simultaneously you have made positive suggestions. She will be "on the carpet" and feel compelled to cooperate with you to work out alternatives. And for this particular problem, you will probably have the principal on your side because he is the person most directly aware of her deficiency in handling her problems. You will be helping him to solve one of his problems with Ms. Cana Handle, a problem that might be difficult for him to discuss with her without parental help.

"Detention again, Johnnie!"

What can I do about a teacher who over-uses detentions— when almost every day she keeps Johnnie after school or in from recess as punishment? A subtle method for handling this would be for you to make several unannounced visits to Ms. Dee Tention, timed so as to keep her there for the conference long after her ordinary dismissal time. If you use this ploy, remember that teachers generally are required to stay after the children are dismissed for a half-hour or an hour. Find out the teachers' dismissal time before you visit so that you time it right.

At this visit, you should wear your friendly pose as you discuss her rationale for keeping children from their play-time. Be relaxed and take your time. If it is apparent that Ms. Tention is trying to end the discussion, don't take her hints; be obtuse. Wear her out. Inquire about other things, Johnnie's progress in various subjects, textbook content, anything to keep her there.

If Dee Tention is even partially perceptive, she will understand your message, because you will have put her in the same place that she keeps putting Johnnie. You'll be teaching her that staying after school is not pleasant when someone else requires it. Talking with parents is part of her job, but she won't like it when it happens on "her time."

If she is direct and tells you that she cannot talk with you right then, claiming to have a "meeting," a favorite escape-excuse used by teachers, say, "This won't take long," and firmly stick to your purpose of detaining her. Drop hints such as, "No one likes to give up his free time, but sometimes even teachers have to stay after school."

Parental Persistence would be more comfortable for some to use from the start; if so, use it. Or you might combine the two:

> YOU: Ms. Tention, keeping Johnnie in from recess so frequently is not working the way you want it to work. You're teaching him that schoolwork is punishment and depriving him of his few chances to let off steam so that he can control himself when he should. I want you to find other ways to help him control his behavior.
>
> DEE TENTION: But Mrs. Parent, this is good behavior-modification procedure. And it works. Johnnie is behaving for me now. [Don't be daunted by her jargon. Behavior modification is the current term for changing the way a child acts by offering rewards and punishments to increase and/or decrease particular behaviors. Behavior-modification instruction teaches stress of rewards for proper behavior; unfortunately, many teachers defend their traditional punishments by calling them behavior modification.]

YOU: It is not good behavior-modification procedure. Behavior modification is supposed to stress positive rewards, not punishment, and the reinforcers (rewards or punishment) are supposed to be intermittent. And you've evidently ignored what is going on inside Johnnie; he is building up tension from your pressure, and I don't like it. He needs at least recess to let off steam. I want you to find ways to reward him; if you are going to use behavior modification, use it correctly.

Ms. TENTION: I can't give him rewards for doing what he is supposed to do. I'd have to do the same for all the other children, and I can't play favorites. [She has informed you that she completely misunderstands behavior modification. It is just an empty term she throws around to impress people.]

YOU: I understand you feel that way, but I want you to review your notes, lectures, and literature on behavior modification, and then come up with positive methods of handling Johnnie and your other students.

Ms. TENTION: [Indignant] I'll have you know, I completely understand behavior modification, and I have had courses in it.

YOU: I'm sure you have had instruction in it, but I want you to review your instruction and find better ways to apply it to Johnnie.

Ms. TENTION: [Huffy] Well, do you have any suggestions? [This is a typical question, often designed to throw you, but it is a good question which you should be prepared to answer.]

YOU: That would depend on each individual thing Johnnie has done to deserve correcting. I cannot give you one simple solution for all problems;

handling children is not easy, and behavior modification is not simple. But I am sure that we can work out appropriate handling of each kind of problem. Now if you will tell me some of the problems, we can deal with each one separately. [She walked into this one by asking for suggestions. She didn't expect answers, but she has committed herself to cooperating with you.]

Ms. TENTION: [Reluctantly] All right, what would you suggest when Johnnie is always giggling with the boy who sits next to him? Those two boys create such a ruckus that the rest of the children cannot get anything done.

YOU: Separate the two boys so that they too can get their work done, and ask yourself if the work they are supposed to be attending to is appropriate. Maybe the work is boring or too difficult.

There are no simple solutions that can be generally applied to handle all classroom problems. Sometimes a teacher over-uses one device for handling all problems. This will not work because the "punishment" degree is not appropriate for all occasions, and generally it loses its effectiveness because of its over-use, and the kids' resistance to the unfairness of it. Sometimes parents have to help teachers with their thinking to explore alternate methods of classroom control.

Unfortunately, most teachers do not get much help from their superiors or associates in working out problems. This is a problem inherent in the profession. Many teachers consider helpful suggestions from administrators or associates as a form of meddling, and they resist it. Because of the antipathy it creates, most educators refrain from making suggestions to their associates. Only parents can fill this vacuum.

"You're not welcome."

If I visit the classroom and the teacher makes it clear, either directly or indirectly, that I am not welcome, what should I do? Hold your ground. The schools belong to the parents and the children, not the teachers. The teacher is your employee, and you pay his salary. You have a right to visit the school, and Mr. Don Visitus would have to get a court injunction to get you out. A good teacher will welcome you; it is only the bad teacher who will try to intimidate you. The teacher is trying to hide something if he doesn't want you there. There is something he is not handling right, and he knows it.

> MR. DON VISITUS: I'm sorry, Mrs. Parent, but this is not a good day to visit; we have so many things scheduled that we won't have time for visitors today. [You're supposed to respond to his problems. Don't!]

> YOU: That's all right. I don't expect any special treatment; just go right on as though I weren't here.

> MR. VISITUS: But Mrs. Parent, it would be disturbing to the children, and we have just too much to get done today. [He has become quite definite about not wanting you. All the more reason to stay.]

> YOU: I'm sure you have a lot to do, and I won't bother the children a bit. They'll be so busy they'll forget my presence. I'll just sit right over there, in that back corner unless you prefer I sit elsewhere. [You have given him no option except your placement.]

> MR. VISITUS: Sit anywhere you like, but you'll be in the way.

> YOU: I'll sit there until you need that area, and I'll move from time to time whenever it appears that I'm in the way. I'm sure I won't bother the children a bit.

Don't be uncomfortable about being there. Mr. Visitus assumed that you, like most people, would not stay where you weren't wanted. Stay as long as you wish, until you've seen what you want to see. The next time drop in unannounced. Several intermittent visits may give you more information than just one visit of long duration. But be certain to stay longer than you wish if Mr. Don Visitus objects to your presence.

"I'll show you!"

What if a teacher viciously begins to take out her anger with me on my child? If a parent tries to do anything about a teacher's behavior, this is a possible consequence. When this happens, you must be prepared to spend even more time at school. Typically, a misbehaving teacher will try to manipulate you by retaliating at least once; unfortunately, this is often all it takes to make many parents back off in fear. Backing off at this point, however, is the worst thing a parent can do.

Instead, go to the building principal and apply Parental Persistence in gaining prevention of the teacher's further misbehavior. This might even mean sitting in the classroom several days, acting as a watchdog to get the information you need and to let her know you will continue to watch her every move until she stops her misbehavior. It is a matter of your having more tenacity than Ms. Reta Liate does. If she is convinced that you will not back off, she is more likely to back off and handle your child very carefully because her job is at stake.

But, if this is not the case, you will have to act to protect your child. Demand that your child be assigned immediately to a different teacher for his own protection.

Use Parental Persistence to accomplish this. Most schools are multiple-unit schools with more than one classroom for each grade, and a transfer of this type can be easily made. Don't be handled with platitudes about "school policy" against changing teachers. You are the customer and the employer who pays both administrators' and teachers' salaries.

> YOU: Mr. Prin Cipal, since I was here last week about Ms. Reta Liate's behavior, things have gotten worse. She has continued her browbeating [slapping, or any specific that applies] of Johnnie, and I want Johnnie transferred to another teacher.

> MR. CIPAL: [Defensive] I talked with Ms. Liate. I doubt that there could be any serious problems. She is a good teacher, Mr. Parent. [He is saying that he cannot control Ms. Liate. He's caught between you and her. Ms. Liate has very likely lied to him, and professionally he is caught in the middle.]

> YOU: I understand that there is a limit to what you can do, but I want Johnnie transferred to a different teacher. Ms. Liate's classroom is an unhealthy place for my boy.

> MR. CIPAL: But Mr. Parent, we can't just transfer kids around to whatever teacher they want or you want. If we did that for you, we'd have to do it for anyone who asked. It's against our policy. [He is loading you with his problems. You have your own problem which you must solve for your child's sake. Don't feel guilty for forcing him to act.]

> YOU: I'm sure that would be a problem, especially if you permit unfit teachers to have full reign, but I insist that Johnnie be transferred immediately to a different teacher.

MR. CIPAL: [Puzzled that you haven't buckled to his manipulations.] Well, I'll see what I can do, but I can't promise anything. . . .

YOU: Good. I'll call you tomorrow at which time I shall expect you to have arranged it. Meanwhile, Johnnie will not spend another day in Ms. Liate's classroom which I consider unsafe for him.

If the principal tries to pass the buck by stating that you must talk with the superintendent or the board, don't do it. That is his job, and that is the run-around tactic designed to wear you out. Say to him: "That is your job, and although it might be difficult for you, I insist that you get the job done whatever way you can." If you take this forceful approach, the principal will probably have the transfer arranged when you call him. He won't like it, but you are interested in what is best for your child, not what the school personnel like or dislike.

TEACH-THE-TEACHER TACTIC

If in the rare instance your persistence does not work, you're still not beaten. If you must, picket the school and the teacher, after you have alerted the local newspaper. Also, by taking your child out of the school, you will be in violation of the state compulsory attendance law, and the authorities will have to come to you to enforce that law. You'll have ample chance to air the school's "dirty laundry" to the courts and newspapers.

But it won't happen that way because there is probably nothing the bureaucratic schools are more afraid of than a public airing of their "dirty laundry." That is why a problem of this magnitude happens only rarely. Someone wins long before this stage of development, either you or the school. Make sure it is you who wins. If you *convince* the teacher and principal at the outset that you will not back down, you will win. You *can* afford to protect your child.

One midwestern couple withdrew all four of their children from the public schools of a large city system because they considered the school a repressive waste of their gifted children's time. The school system quietly kept the action from the newspapers for six weeks as they tried to make arrangements to appease the parents. The embarrassed school system brought no truancy action against the parents. However, a local newspaper finally picked up the story and wrote a full feature article with pictures. The parents, both former educators, were portrayed sympathetically, and the school system was quoted as attempting to find a solution suitable to the parents.

"Now it is time for us all to use the toilet."

What about the teacher who limits toilet trips and water-drinking trips to one scheduled trip midmorning and one midafternoon when all the children "go" at the same time? Fortunately, some schools are abolishing this antiquated system, but there are still many teachers who are so rigid in their control of the children that they insist on uniform toilet times. It is ironic that many children are not given toilet and water-drinking privileges that most adults enjoy at their places of employment. When you "gotta go, you gotta go," and children are no different from adults. There is no reason teachers should expect children to follow restrictions that most adults are not forced to follow, restrictions of biological functions which can be very distressing or physically damaging, if not impossible to abide by.

It is no wonder that children sometimes wet their pants in school. That humiliation is evidently preferable to overcoming fear of a teacher to request permission to use the toilet. Who can say how often anyone else needs to use a toilet or get a drink of water? We all vary considerably in these needs, and the need varies for any individual from one day to another. Suzie doesn't have to put up with this kind of restriction, but only you can do something about it for her. Remember, she is helpless. For toilet and water-drinking privileges, use Parental Persistence to demand that Suzie be given the privileges she needs.

By restricting toilet and water-drinking activities, the teacher has put a premium on these activities, and she has taught the children that even going to the toilet is preferable to studying in that teacher's classroom. This teacher obviously has a low opinion about learning and her classroom particularly. If the premium were removed, after a short time, the children would learn self-control and use toilet privileges with discretion.

3

Teacher-Illiteracy & Other Academic Deficiencies

The old adage, no news is good news, is not necessarily true when it concerns your child's mastering of the three R's. No news means that the school, the teachers, and the administrators are satisfied, but it does not mean that everything is fine—that Johnnie is necessarily learning what he should. Many schools maintain a veil of silence even though very little actual learning is taking place. The mark of a good administrator is one who keeps a low profile, which means that there are few disturbing incidents in the school and absolutely no press coverage concerning anything that does happen—or doesn't happen.

ITEM: In March 1975, the Department of Health, Education, and Welfare revealed that a special study done by the department showed a steady deterioration of reading skills among American students since 1965. The College Entrance Examination Board announced in November 1975 that there had been a twelve-year-long decline in Scholastic Aptitude Test (achievement tests) scores for entering college freshmen. The 1975 scores hit an all-time low.

ITEM: At the University of California at Berkeley, where students come from the top 12.5 percent of high school graduates, in 1974 half of the freshmen were forced to take a remedial English course which is commonly known as "bonehead English."

ITEM: A United States Office of Education study released in October of 1975 revealed that one of every five American adults is "functionally illiterate," lacking the basic know-how to function in our society. This study also found that forty million adults, one in every three, are only minimally competent to function self-sufficiently as citizens, consumers, wage earners or family members. Twenty percent of those in this group did not know the meaning of the words, "We are an Equal Opportunity Employer." Thirteen percent could not address an envelope well enough for the postal service to process it. Fourteen percent could not make out a personal check correctly enough for the bank to process it. Only fifty-five million, fewer than half of this nation's adult population in the age group of eighteen to sixty-five, were proficient in computation and problem-solving skills, reading and writing.

ITEM: The Education Commission of the States, in a 1975 survey of 80,000 students, aged nine, thirteen, and seventeen years old, found a *"remarkable decline"* in writing ability or coherence in youngsters' writing during the last few years.

ITEM: The state of Maryland found that only half of those applying for certification as English teachers could pass a state proficiency examination of the English language.

ITEM: At Temple University in Philadelphia, the number of freshmen failing an English entrance examination has increased by more than 50 percent since 1968.

ITEM: Michigan State University officials, concerned about increasing writing incompetence of its graduates, "may" soon require all degree candidates to pass a writing examination entitled, "Minimal Literary Skills" before they receive their degrees.

ITEM: College textbook publishers are publishing new editions for the purpose of simplifying the reading level and course content to accommodate the new illiterate college generation. In some cases, the reading level of college texts has been reduced to a ninth-grade reading level.

ITEM: Several cities are now setting up "new, experimental, fundamental" schools which will stress the teaching of the three R's. A news article in Des Moines, Iowa, concerning a school proposal states that the district's students "would be given the option next fall of attending the fundamental school which will stress the basic skills such as reading, writing, and arithmetic." The article further states the school's goals: ". . . Place primary emphasis on the teaching of reading, writing, and arithmetic. Develop good, independent study habits. Provide a quiet, orderly learning environment. Build within each child a sense of responsibility, confidence, pride in accomplishment, and a positive self-image through academic achievement. Emphasize discipline and the authority of the teacher."

If these are the goals of a proposed, new fundamental school, one wonders what the goals of the district's fifty other elementary schools are. And when did official policy depart from those "fundamental" goals, at whose request and by whose permission? The tone of the proposal suggests that these goals can be obtained only by a form of teacher tyranny of the children enrolled. The school system plans to require parents to sign a statement saying they agree with the philosophy of the school. This suggests that in exchange for academic achievement parents would be forced to sign away their children's rights, carte blanche. This equating of learning with teacher-tyranny illustrates the attitude of too many educators toward learning.

Why Are All the Standards Falling?

There are many reasons for this, even though all the governmental offices and educational agencies claim that they don't know the reasons. The reasons can be summed up in two words, "attitude" and "survival," the combination of which results in a vicious circle of educational failure to the exclusion of the three R's. Attitude includes teacher militancy and the recent sociological orientation of American education. Survival encompasses the colleges' and universities' efforts to maintain their mammoth educational empires, and the individual faculty members' fight to survive within the institutions at all levels. Teacher incompetence is largely the result of survival tactics in the colleges and universities.

Colleges and universities, overbuilt and overstaffed to educate the post-World War II population explosion, are today crying for students to fill the half-empty classrooms and laboratories. Anyone is accepted for admission today, no matter how low his intelligence or how low his achievement. Survival of the institution has necessitated most of the colleges to lower their standards to accomplish this. Students who would have been flunked out of college during their freshman year ten years ago, are graduating today, many of them with full credentials to teach your children.

Each college instructor wants to preserve his job, and the only way to do this is to keep students. As the student population declines, each department must reduce its staff. "Popular" college teachers keep students happy, hold students, and therefore keep the institution happy and solvent. In order to be popular, college faculties are pressured by their institutions to give high grades "to keep the students."

This national phenomenon is reflected in the inflated grades in all colleges, from Upper Snob U. to Podunk U. Grade inflation has reached the point that even in some of the nation's most prestigious schools over three-fourths of the student body qualifies for the Dean's List. This has prompted a number of colleges to abolish the Dean's List because it has become so meaningless. Grade inflation has been accomplished by lowering standards, if not abolishing them completely. Survival is the name of the game, institutionally and individually.

Naturally, these lower standards have impact on the academic preparation of the new generation of teachers who are now teaching your children. The teacher-training institutions are graduating many people who are virtually illiterate and mathematically incompetent. These graduates will teach your children reading, writing, and arithmetic. With this vicious educational circle, it is no wonder standards continue to deteriorate. These inferior teachers not only are ill-equipped intellectually and academically to educate your child, but also they are caught up in the new teacher militancy and job survival themselves. The result is that your kids will be even less prepared than their teachers were, to function as adults, whether they go on to college or go into the job marketplace.

What Does Attitude Have to Do With It?

Some sociologically oriented teachers today consider academic standards to be "middle-class values." They consider standard English to be a "prestige dialect," contending that standard English is just one of many dialects and that insistence that all children learn it is unfair to those who are not white middle class.

In 1974, after considerable conflict within the organization, the National Council of Teachers of English (NCTE) adopted a policy statement which approved a stance that robs all children of the right to learn standard English. The council did this in an effort to lessen the gap between those children from illiterate backgrounds and those children from literate homes. The NCTE statement entitled "Students' Rights to Their Own Language" argued that:

> Linguistic snobbery was encouraged by a slavish reliance on rules, and these attitudes had consequences far beyond the realm of language. People from different language and ethnic backgrounds were denied social privileges, legal rights, and economic opportunity, and their inability to manipulate the dialect used by the privileged group was used as an excuse for this denial.

But Don't the Disadvantaged Need Special Help?

Of course. Alternate methods and materials are needed. But the disadvantaged need the same skills as the middle-class students. Their parents' lack of these skills is largely the reason these children are disadvantaged. Some educators, like those in the NCTE, evidently do not believe that the purpose of public education is to help those from illiterate backgrounds to learn the necessary skills for surviving in a society that uses those skills in its business, its government, and its everyday communication.

Pulling down those who come from literate backgrounds does not pull up those who do not. The result of this attitude we are seeing today in the low achievement scores in schools everywhere. Educator/sociologists are hiding the illiteracy of some segments of American society by destroying literacy in all groups. They do this by denying literacy training for all children through attitudes like that cited in the NCTE policy statement.

Do-gooders who contend that disadvantaged children cannot and should not learn the competencies of mainstream-America are in reality espousing a pernicious prejudice toward the disadvantaged and/or a profound stupidity. Disadvantaged children have the right and the need to learn the necessary competencies to be responsible, self-supporting citizens within the mainstream. These do-gooder attitudes are condemning the disadvantaged to another generation of disadvantage.

Why Have Educators Allowed This?

The plight of the disadvantaged has been one of the many convenient excuses used by incompetent and lazy teachers for not doing their jobs. By claiming that students have rights to their own language, that computers will do the mathematics, that tapes, typewriters, and TV will do the communicating, teachers have found ready excuses for doing as little as possible. They say they "feel sorry" for the disadvantaged and complain about discipline. These teachers are wasting the students' time, robbing the children of their educational rights, and criminally defrauding the taxpayers who pay their salaries.

Most school systems have no objective method for evaluating applicants for teaching positions. The financial crunch obligates most schools to hire only the minimally trained and inexperienced. Since everyone gets good college grades today, employers cannot even use the grade transcript as a measuring stick. Teachers are hired on such whimsical bases as "a good personality," "our kind," "a winning smile," "good legs" or a "cute ass."

Other professions have state or national examinations that professional candidates must pass *after* they have completed their schooling. Despite graduation from their respective professional schools, lawyers, medical doctors, nurses, architects, certified public accountants, even barbers and cosmetologists, must pass state examinations before they are allowed to practice their professions. Only teachers are allowed to practice without any sort of proficiency examination.

Doesn't the Teaching Profession Police Itself?

That is what the profession tells the public. But the only policing within the educational profession in all but two states is the National Commission for Accreditation of Teacher Education (NCATE), which approves not individual teachers, but the teacher-training institutions. If a training institution meets with the approval of NCATE, then all of that school's graduates are automatically approved on a national basis because of NCATE reciprocity in all states. Of course, NCATE officials are all faculty members of teacher-training institutions. With institutional survival-need to retain and graduate all students, even the most stupid and lazy students, NCATE regulation has become virtually meaningless.

What Can Be Done about This?

Teacher competency examinations are available, but little used. The National Teacher Examination (NTE) published by the Educational Testing Service at Princeton, New Jersey, is presently the most widely used test, but it is required by only two states, Georgia and South Carolina. This examination is available for use by local school systems for screening applicants. Some school systems use this exam, and more should. However, the test publisher sets no passing or failing standards; the standards are set by individual state departments, colleges or school systems who use them. School systems can set the minimum passing score as they wish.

This examination comprises a Common Examination for all teachers and separate exams for the various teaching specialities. The Common Examination tests general education, including written English expression, social studies, science and mathematics, literature and fine arts, and professional education. Separate tests are available in the areas of reading, elementary education, early childhood education, and the various secondary-school subject areas.

There are some who decry tests of this sort, and those who berate them are the very people who are partially responsible for the general lowering of standards with which our schools are now faced. And perhaps they are the very incompetents whom we don't want teaching our children. Incompetence breeds more incompetence when incompetence is the teacher.

It is up to you the parents to demand qualified teachers for your children. And YOU must do it, because neither the teaching profession nor the teacher-training institutions will accept their responsibility to police the competency of those entering the profession.

Through group Parental Persistence, you should demand that your local school district adopt a good standard examination which will assure at least the academic competence of teachers who are hired. A parent-group should also be involved in determining what tests are used and in determining passing and failing scores on such a test. If this is left to the school personnel, you may be very sure that the level set would be so low that virtually all who take the test will pass. The administrators can then continue to hire according to personal whim. And that is exactly what you want to guard against.

Currently, a power struggle is being waged between the teacher-training institutions under the wing of the U.S. Office of Education on one side and the teachers' professional organizations, National Education Association and its state affiliates, on the opposing side. Both sides want control of setting requirements for teacher certification. The conflict centers about who should teach what to teachers-in-training, and how these candidates for teaching certificates should be evaluated for competency. Parents should notice whose interests are not even considered in this power struggle—the children's.

Because everyone in education knows the low state of teacher competency, the U.S. Office of Education recently financed a study and implementation of "Competency Based Teacher Education" (CBTE) in institutions of higher education. The upshot of this effort has been a self-serving proliferation of CBTE programs on college and university campuses. CBTE sounds good in concept, but because of fadism and a race for federal money, it has evolved in nonstandard, nonobjective, non-evaluated, and nonresearched ways. The profusion of wildly different programs all call themselves "competency-based."

Critics of CBTE, including professional teacher associations, contend that CBTE reduces teaching from an intelligent, thoughtful application of sound educational theory, to a "trade" concerned only with the unthinking mastering of certain techniques learned by rote, techniques which are neither understood nor tested in practice. This inhuman approach treats all children as though each child were identical to every other child—assembly-line items to be processed in a nonvarying, prescribed manner. There is justifiable concern that CBTE programs are at wide variance with each other, are lacking in research-based criteria and in evaluation techniques.

This is the battle which the public's dissatisfaction with the schools brought about within the educational fraternity. But the public has no part in it, knows little about it, and doesn't feel it understands it. The truth of the matter is that neither side of the conflict really has the improvement of education as its chief concern—no matter the idealistic lip service it gives to education. Motivation on both sides is self-interest in maintaining the status quo.

How Is That?

CBTE programs as they have evolved on many campuses amount to little more than a subterfuge for the lowering of standards in order for the teacher-training institutions to retain virtually all nonthinking students. This is to maintain the empire and sustain funding of the school, whether public or private. CBTE programs rely very heavily on "experience" types of training which cannot be objectively evaluated, and laborious, programmed-methods-training which is spoon-fed and evaluated, if at all, in parrot fashion. Many programs are a hodgepodge of memorized minutiae which ignore the concepts of comprehension and assimilation, both of which are crucial for the intelligent teacher who must think on her feet, and adapt material and methods for individual children.

Criticism of CBTE programs by professional teacher organizations are, on the surface, justified and sound. But the major motivation for this criticism goes much deeper than the surface criticism. Teachers do not want to be evaluated in *any* way. Teachers have successfully resisted evaluation for years because those responsible for setting up procedures for this are all members of the teaching profession.

The teacher surplus, which continues largely because of the lowering of standards of colleges and universities, is viewed as a threat to those already holding teaching certificates. For the first time, the interests of employed teachers are opposite to the interests of teacher-training institutions. The name of the game is jobs, not education.

"Accountability" is a relatively new term that has found its way into education during the last few years. This concept, which is still in its infancy, is not liked by most educators because it means that the public is demanding that teachers prove the worth of their work. But accountability set into motion the CBTE conflict within education. The public is beginning to ask the school what it is accomplishing and to show results. The stage is now set for parental demands on the schools.

If the public will utilize the concept of accountability and make it work, parents and children will not have to put up with the incompetence, indifference, snippiness, and brutality of teachers. Recently, the concept of accountability has found its way into laws of some twenty-three states. These laws are requiring the development of assessment programs and evaluation systems. Reporting procedures or public disclosure to the citizens is also part of these laws. But the public should be involved in developing accountability procedures so that the educators don't get away with complying with the letter of the law but not complying with the intent of the law. Educators will circumvent the intent of the law if parents permit it.

Presently, California and eight other states have enacted teacher-competency acts. The California act stipulates that four factors must be included in evaluation. These are: expected student progress, preserving a suitable environment, and maintaining proper control and other duties normally required as adjunct to regular assignments. Emphasis is on "expected" student progress. Laws set precedents, but the public must insist that the laws be enforced and interpreted, not as the teachers and the teacher-training institutions wish, but as the public wishes. It's your move!

Until standards can be changed, you will have to find individual ways to assure that your Johnnie and your Suzie are given the academic skills they need.

Is There One Major, All-Pervasive Academic Problem?

Inflexibility of teachers to adapt methods and adopt materials according to the various learning styles of children is the chief problem. We call this the "Oatmeal" philosophy, which goes something like this: "We feed all the kids oatmeal (or Sparkle Puffs, if the school is progressive), which is good for all children. If your kid doesn't thrive on oatmeal, something is wrong with your child. But all we have at this school is oatmeal, and your child is going to have to learn how to eat it or starve. So we'll feed him a little at a time until he learns to tolerate it, no matter how allergic he is to oatmeal or how much weight he loses in the meantime." "Oatmeal" might be the Sullivan Programmed Reading series or it might be the Ginn Reading Series.

The current popularization of behavior-modification techniques, to the exclusion of all other learning theories, lends itself beautifully to the "oatmeal" philosophy. If behavior-modification is the only learning method known or used by subscribers to the "oatmeal" philosophy, they will either reward Johnnie with one piece of candy for every bite of oatmeal he eats or they will crack Johnnie across the mouth for every bite of oatmeal he refuses or spits out. A different diet is never considered. Oatmeal is all!

If it is suggested that Johnnie might adapt better to another diet, the schoolmarms may say, "If you insist on another diet for Johnnie, we cannot be responsible for it, and he'll have to find the food himself, fix the food, and decide for himself how to prepare it, how much of it to eat, and whether or not it agrees with him."

What can I do if the school insists on serving only oatmeal even if Johnnie is allergic to it? Explain to the teacher that the diet she is serving Johnnie is not working. He is not gaining any weight (academic achievement) or that he is allergic to it (Johnnie isn't learning by this method, and he is developing anxiety, aggressiveness, hostility, whatever) because nothing else is served him. If the teacher is intelligent and well-educated, she will take the suggestion positively and will devise an alternative diet for Johnnie. She might decide to use different textbook material, shifting from a programmed text to a basal reader, or use a different motivation system, or find an achievement level at which Johnnie can adequately function. If you have a good teacher, she'll recognize the validity of your suggestion and make an effort. But it is too bad that you yourself have to be the one to recognize this kind of problem to get any remediation.

But, if the teacher is defensive, stupid, or lazy, she will attempt to defend oatmeal and in the process very likely imply that "teacher knows best." Don't be put off by this kind of manipulation. If you are convinced that what the school is using to teach Johnnie hasn't worked and isn't working, don't waste any more of Johnnie's time.

> YOU: I understand that you feel the way you do, but I want a different approach (text, materials, whatever) used for Johnnie.

> MS. OATMEAL: But Mrs. Parent, the Sullivan program is one of the best programs used today.

> YOU: I'm sure it is, but not for Johnnie. I want a different program for him. [Don't argue the merits of various approaches with her; that is a trap to defeat you. And don't leave until she agrees to look into alternative approaches. Set a time limit and date for your inspection of the program.]

What if I really don't know anything about reading programs—or whatever? Fine. Most people don't know about these things. That is why we hire teachers. There are two routes you can go from here. You can have the teacher explain at least one alternative method of teaching reading to you, how it is different from what she is using, what the advantages and disadvantages are, and which kind of kids respond better to which kind of approach. Or you can hire an experienced teacher who is unemployed (there are many these days), or a teacher who is in no way associated with your school system. Have this experienced teacher, preferably a reading consultant, suggest alternatives for you to present to Johnnie's teacher. Make sure you get a teacher who is in no way connected with your local school system because no employee is allowed to criticize oatmeal.

If your county or area education office is a service-type office, you might be able to consult free of charge with a reading consultant who could determine the best program to present to the teacher. Remember one thing; don't let the school get away with the Oatmeal philosophy. If it hasn't worked for Johnnie before, it won't work later. You care about Johnnie's academic progress; you can only hope his teacher does.

What about all the teacher aides, associates, and volunteers in many schools these days? From the close of World War II until 1965, over-burdened teachers with far too many children assigned per classroom did their jobs valiantly and courageously. They knew they had too many kids assigned to them, but they knew there was a critical shortage of teachers available. Those teachers of the fifties and sixties had a tough job to do, and they did it. A look at high national achievement test scores of that period tells how well they did their job.

Those teachers asked for help in the form of teacher-aides since they knew that enough certified teachers were not available. But they did not get much help. No one heard their plea, and so they courageously did the best they could.

Times changed, and the teacher-shortage turned into a teacher-surplus as the post–World War II baby boom was graduated from college. As the teacher-surplus was created, so was double-digit inflation and financial problems for the schools. Overburdened school boards and taxpayers remembered the old plea for teacher-aides and discovered that by hiring some of these cheaper, untrained persons, the school system could get by without hiring quite so many qualified teachers. The teacher-aide concept was "discovered" and declared a marvelous new concept in education. The public, which is always ready to save a buck, bought the concept and told themselves the story that this was good.

But no one asked what was good about hiring unqualified help when every community has many unemployed teachers available who need jobs. And no one asked what would happen to the quality of education in the classrooms when the schools were hiring more and more untrained persons to work with the children under the direction of "cheap" inexperienced certified teachers. Perhaps this is a large part of the reason academic achievement has slipped so much in the last few years.

Ironically, as many of those valiant teachers of the fifties and early sixties are retiring or standing in un-employment lines, the new militant teachers are receiving the help, at government expense, of teacher-aides. The same power-happy generation which bombed the college campuses and shouted "down with the establishment" are gaining control of the classrooms with the inept assistance of teacher-aides. That is, those of that generation who are able to get teaching jobs.

Who is getting ripped off? The kids, of course. As usual.

If volunteers, teacher-aides, or teacher-associates are teaching my child academic subjects, what should I do? It is illegal in most states. Check the state school code or call the nearest state or county education office to find out. If you telephone, listen carefully for clues to the run-around, because these offices devote themselves to protect-ing the schools. They don't want any trouble, and parents generally are viewed as potential trouble. Press them to read the state code to you on this point. Through your lo-cal library or via interlibrary loan from the state univer-sity, you can also get the information you want.

Although it is illegal for noncertified personnel to teach, volunteerism has gotten out of hand in some school systems, either intentionally to save money by hiring cheaper help, or unethically because teachers through la-ziness are assigning nonlicensed persons to do their jobs for them.

The teaching of arithmetic, reading, or any academic subject is limited to licensed teachers, persons who hold valid teaching certificates. In most states, aides, associates, and volunteers can be used only for nonteaching jobs, such as grading papers, keeping records, putting on boots, and helping to supervise students only when a teacher is present. However, the line between these jobs and the actual teaching is a difficult line to observe. Some schools do a good job of this, but others completely ignore the differentiation, permitting noncertified personnel to do everything the teachers do.

If there is flagrant violation of the law, you should gather proof, submit it to the school board, and demand that a qualified teacher be hired to replace the untrained person or require the teacher already there to do her job. To get proof, you might spend a day or two observing and tape-recording the noncertified person teaching. A cassette with a condenser mike does fine for this. If you have proof of this type and threaten a lawsuit, the school board members will trip over each other trying to correct the problem.

By the time the school hires large numbers of untrained associates, it is paying more money to unqualified help than it would have had to spend for a few good qualified teachers. There is no shortage of certified teachers today. Some classrooms become so cluttered with volunteers, aides, and associates, that the teacher spends all of her time directing her empire. The children in such a classroom never receive direct instruction from a qualified teacher. The children, of course, do not know the difference between teachers and aides. Children assume that anyone teaching them is a teacher. A great deal of misguided, ignorant, defeating instruction is given to innocent children by these well-intentioned, unqualified people.

Kids with academic problems are routinely assigned to aides and volunteers. The children who have not responded to a certified teacher's methods, the children who need the most expert specialists, are the ones assigned to the totally unqualified volunteer for individual help. It is no wonder so few kids respond to so-called "remedial" programs. This is especially true of some federally subsidized programs; these programs do little more than reduce unemployment among the unskilled.

"Pianos are good flyers" for "Peonies are good flowers."

What if I discover that Johnnie simply cannot read material which should be well within his ability? Go to the school and look at Johnnie's permanent records. Find out what his scores are on reading achievement tests. And then find out how he got these scores if his scores indicate average or passing achievement when you know he cannot read. Look over his past report cards and see what they have been indicating about his reading. If you haven't been given any notification of his having a reading difficulty, there is something wrong. If either the report cards or the reading test scores indicate there is no problem, then the school has been cheating Johnnie and deceiving you to cover up the school's failure to teach Johnnie. This is a very common tactic used by teachers to make themselves look good and to keep parents at a distance.

Tackle the teacher and the principal to point out the discrepancy between Johnnie's purported achievement and what you know to be the actual case. Force them to see the problem by showing them material which you know he cannot read.

Ask them what they have been doing to help Johnnie with his reading problem. If they haven't recognized that he has a reading problem or if they sheepishly acknowledge that they knew it, but haven't done anything about it, ask them what kinds of remedial reading programs they have available in the school system. Insist that an evaluation of his reading problems be made by a qualified diagnostician and that an appropriate remedial problem be started for Johnnie immediately.

Don't be put off by phony assurances that everything

will be "all right" or that they are doing everything they can or even that they will "look into it." Nail them down to a specific course of action through Parental Persistence.

> YOU: Regardless of test scores, Johnnie is not able to read this simple material I've shown you. Now, I want a remedial program planned for Johnnie.

> PRINCIPAL: But Mrs. Parent, you've got to give him time. These things come slowly for some. You'd be surprised at how some of these kids take off when they get into the swing of things.

> YOU: I understand you feel that way, but Johnnie is not "slow," and I want something done about his reading now.

> TEACHER: But Mrs. Parent, [lecturing a child] we don't believe in pushing the children. It is not our philosophy to lead them to failure.

> YOU: I know you don't want to push Johnnie, but I insist that you give him suitable help to bring his reading up to his potential.

> TEACHER: Do you know what you are doing to your child by driving him? [This is the guilt hook. Don't grab it.]

> YOU: I know that Johnnie needs to learn to read, and I insist that you do something about it.

> PRINCIPAL: [Resigned] Well, maybe we could get that reading consultant from the county office to help us set up something. Don't you suppose so, Miss Brooks?

> YOU: That will be fine. How soon can you get this done?

PRINCIPAL: I'll check with the consultant tomorrow and set up an appointment as soon as possible.

YOU: Good, I'll call you the day-after-tomorrow to find out the details.

Your child has a right to learn to read if he has normal intelligence. Although 99 percent of the population has experienced elementary-school training in the United States, 20 percent of the adult population is functionally illiterate. The schools have not done their job because the parents have allowed the schools to get away with it. In the last couple of years, a few parents have become fed up with it and a few have even gone to court and sued the schools for graduating people who cannot read. You must make sure Johnnie gets the help he needs. A variety of professionals are available, depending on the cause and type of problem. The chapters on professionals and special education deal with remedial reading—a subject often beyond the knowledge of the ordinary classroom teacher.

"Jump into the pool, Suzie, before we fill it with water."

Why does a teacher insist that Suzie learn a complicated skill before she has been taught the basic skills on which it is based—such as the multiplication table when she hasn't yet been taught to add? Stupidity is the only answer to that. You as a parent know that before a child can understand how to multiply, he must know how to count by twos, threes, fours, etc. If this kind of sequencing hasn't been done for your child, you should find some workbooks which teach this to Suzie, or you should teach her how to do it yourself. This is really not a difficult thing to teach, and it makes the multiplication table much easier. Only lack of knowledge and lack of use of this concept makes the multiplication table difficult for children to learn.

Some children cannot learn this concept without contact with manipulative objects. This does not mean that the child has a learning problem; it means that the thing just never made any sense to him. Buttons, pennies, anything can be used for this. A marvelous device for teaching multiplication is a piece of pegboard with ten holes in each direction, and some sawed-off golf tees. By using this, you can show the child how two pegs in each of two rows equal four pegs, $2 \times 2 = 4$; three pegs in each of two rows equal 6, or $3 \times 2 = 6$. Multiplication makes sense to children, and you can do it at home if the teacher is too stupid to do it.

How can Johnnie learn to tell time when the school hasn't yet taught him to count to sixty by fives? He can't. In order to learn to tell time, Johnnie needs to know that there are five minutes between each number on a clock, and he needs to learn how to count to sixty by fives. Then you begin to teach him how to use the hands of the clock to tell time.

You can buy all kinds of cute devices for teaching a child how to tell time, but really all you need is one good clock that has distinctively different minute and hour hands and no second hand. The face of a good clock has all twelve Arabic numbers on it and preferably has minute marks between the numbers. Then you teach Johnnie to count by fives around the clock to sixty.

Telling time is a rather difficult skill to teach, and it should be sequenced over about the first three grades. Unfortunately, sometimes a kindergarten teacher will try to teach it all at once, or a second-grade teacher will decide that Johnnie should know it all in her class, even though he has had no preparation for it in kindergarten or first grade. Some schools need better sequencing within the school. One little second-grade boy was badgered by a student-teacher who made up her mind that she was going to teach the boy how to tell time in one day—even if it took all day. She wouldn't allow him to go out for recess or do any other work during that day. He did not learn to tell time, but he learned to hate clocks and avoided learning to tell time for two years after this event.

"We're 'individualized' here. Do Book II again, Johnnie."

*What about the school which is a so-called "individualized"
school that wants to start Suzie over again every year—
without officially flunking her?* This is one of the serious
problems that exists in the "individualized" school. It is
a problem that is not easily recognized by parents because
the individualization hides discrepancies between what a
child should be doing and what he is doing. Individualization can allow a child to drop further and further behind
without knowing it.

When teachers keep starting a child over, whether
in the same materials or in comparable materials, you can
be reasonably sure the teacher doesn't know what to do
and/or is practicing the Oatmeal philosophy. A friend's
son was having difficulty with a programmed reading
book and did not learn through use of this material. His
mother, an experienced elementary teacher, asked the
teacher to teach to the boy's deficit in this area. When the
mother next checked, she found that the teacher had made
very poor, unreadable dittoed copies of the same programmed book that the boy had already completed with
no success; the boy was doing the same material again,
but this time he was using fuzzy, unreadable copies. This
was the teacher's solution for a boy who was having
reading problems. The least this teacher could have done
was to transfer the boy into another reading series which
covered the competencies the boy needed.

Much of education is reviewing, using skills already
attained and slowly adding to these skills. A good teacher will isolate the particular problem areas, teach to them
on an individual basis, and keep the child building his
skills. It is very discouraging always to be starting over
and having to plow through all the same garbage again
whether it is needed or not. Most children, and most
adults, view this as punishment. Adequate teaching constantly contains review. Even if the child has not quite

"got it together," with a little extra help, he has a chance of "getting it together" when he gets the next piece of the "puzzle."

If the school wants to hold Suzie back a year—flunk her—should I agree? Don't hold still for it, and for goodness sake, don't suggest it yourself. If Suzie did not learn the material for that grade this year from that teacher, she is not going to learn it next year from the same teacher—and probably not from a different . teacher. Suzie would be busy trying to adjust to a younger age group, busy trying to salvage her damaged self-concept, and she won't have time to learn anything. To Suzie, everything that is done in the repeated grade will just be the same old garbage which baffled and defeated her before; she won't devote any effort to it.

Research on flunking children or holding them back shows that repeating a grade does not help the child academically. The research further shows that repeating a grade can do great social and psychological damage.

This child needs some kind of special help. The Oatmeal diet didn't work the first time; it won't work the second time. See the chapter on special education for kinds of resources that could help Suzie.

"Ho hum, another programmed text."

What about the child who is bored with school? This child may be a very intelligent child who has been assigned to doing routine, repetitive tasks which are not at all challenging to him. Many bright children are bored in schools that use nothing but programmed instruction materials. Programmed instructional materials are purposely designed for the least intelligent child in that grade. Programmed materials inch along at a snail's pace, moving only one small step at a time, making no provision for intuitive leaps. Naturally, bright children are bored with this kind of learning. About the only thing these children are learning is that learning is a bore, which is a sad thing for a bright child. Using programmed materials for all children in the school is another example of the Oatmeal philosophy.

The situation calls for Parental Persistence to insist that the teachers find materials that are more challenging and more interesting for the child. There is no end to the variety of reading materials at all levels for bright children. The only excuse for lack of variety of suitable materials in a classroom is the teacher's laziness or her reluctance to vary her act. Varied materials will make more work for the teacher, but that is her problem. Your job is to see to it that Suzie's interest in learning and her intellectual curiosity are not turned off before she has had a chance to learn about the wonders of exploration.

Teachers who are lazy or lacking creativity can kill a child's interest in any subject—reading, science, mathematics, or any other. One of the chief crimes against intelligent children is that we bore them for four or five years and then we sometimes want to put them into "gifted" programs, and by then all they have learned is how not to study.

"Johnnie's IQ score proves that he cannot learn."

What should be done when the school tells me that my child is failing to achieve because he has a low IQ? View test scores with suspicion. Many students appear to have a low intelligence when they do not because of improper testing, caused by inadequate tests, poor testing conditions, improper motivation, and many other physical and environmental factors. Some teachers and administrators have had horribly inadequate training in the use of tests; it is their ignorance and abuse of tests which have given the tests a bad name and have resulted in condemning many people to totally unsuitable education.

Check the source of the IQ score that influences such

an important decision. Is the test a "group" intelligence test? If so, do not accept this score as proof of anything. Does the school base its decision on only one test? If so, the school is misusing test scores. Group intelligence test scores are invalid for people who cannot read. If a person cannot read well, a low score measures reading, not IQ. Tests are equally invalid for the kid who felt bad, either physically or psychologically, the day he took the test. If a student is not motivated, a group test is invalid. If a person "clutches" on tests or has generalized high anxiety, a group test is meaningless.

The only IQ test score to which parents should give any consideration is a properly administered individual test, the Wechsler Intelligence Scale for Children (WISC) or the Stanford-Binet for young children, and the Wechsler Adult Intelligence Scale (WAIS) for teenagers and adults. Most school children have not taken these individual tests. Many school systems require parental permission to administer an individual test to a child.

If a school is deciding Johnnie's fate on the basis of IQ test scores, you should get more information about Johnnie's ability, his strengths and weaknesses. Parents who have this problem should be sure to read the remaining chapters on tests, professionals, and special education before authorizing any further testing. Proper evaluation will take time, and no snap decisions should be made.

No matter what the results of any testing, parents should demand appropriate education for their child. It is not fair to any child simply to let him slide through the regular school program without learning anything, especially the child who has learning problems.

Low scores on intelligence tests are a convenient excuse that educators have used for not doing their jobs. The teacher's job is to meet the child where he is, academically and intellectually, and give him training to realize his potential. Excusing poor achievement by crying "low potential" is one of the most common cop-outs used by the schools. If an educator tunes into a low IQ score, he tends not to expect much from the student, very often gives no pertinent aid, and, therefore, the student doesn't achieve very much.

Self-fulfilling prophecy simply means that we tend to perform as we expect ourselves to perform; and that expectation of ourselves is generally determined by what others expect of us. If not much is expected of us, we don't produce much. If a great deal is expected of us, we tend to produce more. There has been a lot of research done on this topic in recent years, and the research all bears out the validity of self-fulfilling prophecy.

"Do as I say, not as I do."

What about the teacher who insists that young Johnnie hold his pencil in the prescribed Palmer Method manner? The Palmer Method of holding a pencil is anatomically impossible. Ask the teacher for a demonstration of her writing; ask her if she holds the pencil in that manner when she writes. There is no question about it; she will not hold her pencil in the Palmer manner. No one does. Yet daily in hundreds of classrooms throughout this country, children are still being forced to try to write in this anatomically impossible way.

Young children learn very effectively through modeling; if Ms. Imo Schizo cannot model this behavior, then she has no business teaching it. She should not be teaching contradictions. If Ms. Schizo pleads school-administration jurisdiction here, then use Parental Persistence to insist that she make an exception of your child because of the impossibility of the Palmer Method. Don't allow your child to be led to a feeling of failure at the young age when he is learning how to hold a pencil. The schools have thousands of future opportunities to make him feel he is a failure. Put your instruction on this matter in writing if the teacher is weak and wishes protection.

"Johnnie is in the vocational program; he doesn't need to learn to read or do arithmetic."

What does it mean when the school is not teaching Johnnie basic academic skills because they have put him in a "vocational" or "career" program? This depends on how old Johnnie is and which basic skills are being neglected. If Johnnie is in elementary school and he is not learning the three R's, you have a legitimate complaint. But if Johnnie is in high school and he is not studying trigonometry, he might be better off. At the high-school level, the choice between career education and academic education depends on several factors, the intellectual-ability level of the student, the student's interests, his achievement and his attitude toward school.

Even though you as a parent might agree with the school that career education is probably appropriate for Johnnie, there are certain basic skills that all people need for any vocation and just to be operative in our society. These include reading, writing, and arithmetic. There is no defense for a school declaring vocational or career education the right course for Johnnie and promptly quitting on the basic three R's that everyone needs.

A good carpenter, mechanic, plumber, dental hygienist, secretary, all need to know how to read, write, and do arithmetic. There is no way a person can produce in the work world, if he survives at all, anywhere near his potential if he doesn't have those skills.

Yet, some schools in their ignorance are using the popular term "career" education as an excuse for not teaching reading and arithmetic to kids even down in fourth and fifth grades. These kids are generally the kids who have been having a rough time learning those skills, and in many cases these are intelligent kids. Twenty percent of the adult population, ages twenty-five through sixty-five, is functionally illiterate.

If you see this happening to your child, apply Parental Persistence to get those skills taught to him in order that he may survive. You know what "operative level" means in terms of reading and arithmetic, and you can insist that these be taught until that point is reached by your child. It doesn't matter if Johnnie is reading comic books and Suzie is reading romance magazines, as long as they are reading. They don't have to be reading classics or any of the books that the bookish declare suitable. Algebra and geometry are not necessary for all to learn, but everyone must know how to add, subtract, multiply, and divide.

Career education is so misunderstood by the education profession that as the schools adopt this basically good concept, large proportions of the students are being denied adequate basic skills for the sake of what is becoming, unfortunately, another gimmick in the schools. Most teachers haven't the slightest idea of what career education or vocational education involves, but it is the teachers who are designing the programs. Many educators view these terms as new names for programs for the stupid, and many other educators have lived so far removed from the world of work that they will teach your child from their own story-book idealization of other careers.

If you've got this kind of thing going in your school, you probably will have to mobilize a committee of self-appointed parents to petition the school board to teach the basics to your kids before it is too late. If the basics are not even available in your school, you'll have to use Parental Persistence as a group in dealing with your school board.

Some school systems have organized advisory boards composed of various occupations from the community to help with career and vocational programs. This is good, but in some communities, these advisory boards are handled by the schools to the point that the advisory board is a rubber stamp for what the educators want to do, or the advisory board is ignored. Educators are inherently reluctant to allow lay persons to contribute much meaningful input. The program is designed by educators, and the mechanics, plumbers, and so on, are asked to approve the program. Skilled craftsmen generally approve programs as requested out of modesty, believing that the educators know what they are doing.

How should I react when the school says that Suzie is "not motivated?" Motivation to learn is inborn. A child's chief pursuit is learning—satisfying his curiosity. But something happens when he goes to school; all of a sudden he turns off. Isn't it odd that the school is the place that thwarts intellectual curiosity?

Academic motivation is largely the responsibility of the school. If the school tells you that Suzie is not motivated, then you should tell them that the teachers are not presenting the materials in the right way or that the material is wrong. The teachers must change the method of presentation or the materials they are presenting. There is a multitude of teaching materials on the market, and most school systems have on hand more than one type of material. If a variety of these materials is not used, it is simply a matter of the teachers being too lazy to pick up a knowledge of the alternative materials that are often already in the school.

You might get a "not motivated" report at a regular conference. If you do, you should be prepared to handle it on the spot.

> MS. UNA MOTIVATED: Suzie is really not doing as well as she could. I really don't think she is motivated. She doesn't seem interested in what she is doing.

> YOU: Do you suppose it is the materials she is not interested in, or is it the way it is presented that turns her off? [You've thrown it in her lap.]

MS. UNA MOTIVATED: [Flustered because she has never thought it might be her fault.] She's just not motivated. She's not interested. [She didn't answer your question. She doesn't want to deal with it. She's depending on you to take her off the griddle. Don't.]

YOU: Which do you think it is? [Keep her on the subject.]

MS. UNA MOTIVATED: [Anger darting from her eyes as she speaks.] I think Suzie has a lot of problems that preoccupy her. [She's taking the blame off herself and putting it on you. Don't bite on that one.]

YOU: Suzie doesn't have any problems. She's just bored with school. You said so yourself. Now, we want you to devise some method of stimulating her academic interest.

MS. UNA MOTIVATED: Well, I don't know. I have thirty other students. [Now she has shifted to "feel sorry for me." Don't buy it. Nobody said that a teacher's job should be easy.]

YOU: Are you capable of exploring Suzie's special interests with her, finding suitable materials and experimenting with other teaching methods? [You've put her on. How can she answer this with a "no"?]

MS. UNA MOTIVATED: Why, of course, but...

YOU: Then we want you to explore some ideas and talk with us again—in, say a week from today. Will that be all right?

MS. UNA MOTIVATED: [Bewildered] Yes, I suppose so.

"Brainwashing instead of social studies."

What if Johnnie spouts only one side of a controversial issue as fact and cites the school as the source? He could be pro or anti: abortion, communism, drug use, race, or any other highly controversial topic, not in keeping with your family's views. You and some other parents in your neighborhood of like conviction should spend some time visiting that classroom. If you find that opinion is being taught as fact by a teacher, fear not to challenge the opinion. No teacher has a right to blatantly teach his opinion as fact to your children. When you visit this classroom, take a tape recorder with you to have accurate records. If the teacher is clever enough to not present his propaganda when you visit, have your son or daughter take a small tape recorder to class to tape the discussions you want recorded.

No parent has to allow his child to be propagandized contrary to the views of the parents. A number of parent groups have demanded that their views on controversial matters be respected by the schools. In Lombard, Illinois, in 1970, a parent group organized and devised a form entitled "Notice of Parental Rights" which instructed the school of individual students' rights to avoid blatant propaganda. These parents served individual notices on the school which demanded the students' rights to remove themselves from any class in which they were exposed to indoctrination and to report to the parents promptly any disregard of their rights.

What if Suzie seems to be spending a lot of time in school on controversial or "popular" topics to the exclusion of the basics that should be taught? These topics are very good learning vehicles, but if the children are not being taught the basic survival skills they need to be operative in the society, the children are robbed of their individual rights as citizens. These children cannot do much as adults to solve the environmental or racial problems if they do not learn to read, write, and do arithmetic. A nation of functional incompetents cannot solve the world's problems. Teachers who neglect the basics to stress other topics are placing the cart before the horse.

This might be the time for you to ask to see Suzie's achievement test scores (reading, math, history, etc.) to check the growth rate. It might be the time to check on the school's and school system's average achievement test scores. If the important skills are not taught, over a period of time, these scores will not grow for individual children, and the system's average score will erode over a period of time. And most are these days. A system's achievement score class averages should register actual academic growth as a class moves from grade five to grade six.

You should go to the teacher and the principal and say that these enrichment topics are very nice, but not at the expense of academic subjects. As an example, suppose that you believed an American history class was being mishandled:

> MR. PRINCIPAL: Mr. and Mrs. Parent are concerned about the amount of emphasis you are giving race relations in your American history class, Mr. Story.

> MR. STORY: Yes, we've been studying the U.S. laws regarding segregation, but I don't understand...

> YOU: We are concerned about the great amount of time you are spending on this topic because you are neglecting all the rest of American history. So far, you have spent nine weeks on segregation. This is a disproportionate amount of time, considering the great volume of material which makes up American history.

> MR. STORY: It's impossible to teach all of American history in a one-year survey course. I'm trying to

make the course relevant. [He side-stepped the issue.]

YOU: I understand that it is difficult to teach all of American history in a one-year survey course, and that is exactly why we want you to spend appropriate amounts of time on each topic so that at least the highlights of American history can be touched upon.

MR. STORY: But desegregation is an important part of American history. Don't you believe in desegregation? [He has called you a bigot; he wants you to get angry, and he is trying to channel the discussion away from his error.]

YOU: Desegregation is a part of American history, but a small part. We want you to teach our child about the many historical facts and issues in our rich, American history.

MR. STORY: The kids are interested in this. It's relevant. [He wants to avoid the issue and argue with you about "his stuff."]

YOU: I understand that it is relevant, but it is not the whole of American history which you were hired to teach, and we want you to teach the whole of American history.

MR. PRINCIPAL: Surely you are about done with your unit on desegregation, aren't you, Mr. Story? [He's finding a compromise.]

MR. STORY: Yes, we finish it at the end of this week.

A great deal was gained by this transaction. You made it clear to both the teacher involved and the administration that you do not condone this kind of teacher distortion of course content and have warned the administration that the public has authority to police education of the youth. From this simple interchange, a teacher will be cautious about this kind of subversion of the basics of your child's education. Such distortion of course content might account for part of the decline of achievement test scores for more than a decade.

"All the children are below grade-level these days; don't worry about it."

What if Johnnie's scores on achievement tests are not showing adequate growth from year to year? Ask to see the chart of the school average or system average, which shows the kind of growth that is being made by all the children. If the charts of the system-wide average do not appear to show growth, then the school could be spending too much time on so-called enrichment or "creative" activities to the detriment of the basics. This could also reflect over-reliance on programmed texts which move at a snail's pace. Monotonous programmed materials are not only a crashing bore to intelligent children but also they fail to allow the children to progress very rapidly. Probably excessive attention to small-step minutiae in programmed materials is partly responsible for the lowering of national achievement test scores.

If the problem is system-wide, not limited to just one classroom or one school, group parental action will be needed to correct this problem. A self-appointed group of parents should approach the local board of education to demand the board's revision of policy on emphasis or methods within the curriculum.

"Academic achievement is irrelevant."

What if the school system decides to throw out the standard achievement tests with excuses such as irrelevancy or expense? This, too, calls for parents to pressure the school board into insisting that these tests be given. This has been done by parents in a number of communities successfully. Again, an unofficial, self-appointed group of parents should band together to petition the board to turn the curriculum completely around so that it conforms to what you, the parents, want for your children. This can be accomplished in a relatively short time, within two or three months. This action could salvage for your child two or three years of academic loss, so that he is more ready to function whether in further education or in a job.

Many educators are very willing to throw out achievement tests, because they see these instruments as a measurement or evaluation of the teaching that goes on. And, to a great extent, they are just that. Your high taxes are supporting expensive schools which should produce. The only objective measure of school production is the achievement test. If the school can throw out the measuring devices, no one can know what teaching is being done, what learning is going on until years later when it is too late for the children concerned.

Isn't there a place for creative inquiry in the school? Yes, but not to the neglect of basic skills. A school based on "wholesale creativity" is not a school at all. The proper time for creativity in many fields is after the basics are learned. A surgeon must first master the basics of anatomy and surgery before attempting creative brain surgery. It would be catastrophic if he attempted creative surgery *instead* of learning the basics which years of research have compiled. It is equally catastrophic for the schools to be so creative that your child is robbed of the basic skills you know he will need to survive. A truly creative teacher is able to intersperse creativity within the framework of the basics the children need. An occasional "brainstorming" session is healthy education, but a steady diet of it neglects adequate schooling.

What are some of the clues to teacher-neglect of the basic skills? Talk with your Johnnie and Suzie. What are they doing in school? How much writing are they doing? How much reading are they doing? How much math are they actually computing? Or are they spending all their time listening to tapes, watching films and television, discussing these things, and spending several days outdoors doing "field problems" such as measuring the football field, which might result in only one simple math computation?

It is legitimate to study via these techniques as enrichment application of the basics, but far too many teachers get carried away with the gimmickry and neglect fundamental skill-building your kids will need. It's fun, it's easy, and the kids love it, but not much learning goes on.

If a language teacher works with the kids on basic writing skills, shows a film and then has the students individually organize their ideas and then write about the film, the teacher is using the film. But if the teacher never teaches writing skills, but shows films and has the kids discuss them, then that teacher has made her job very easy by robbing your child of the ability to write.

What if Johnnie is enrolled in a "career program" for which there is no apparent job opportunity? This happens all the time, and it has to do with vested interests. Yes, there are vested interests even in the public schools. Many teachers of increasingly obsolete skills such as cabinetmaking, shorthand, bookkeeping, defend the career value of these skills because their jobs, their careers, are at stake. If the truth were well-known about the career value of some of these "vocational" courses, those teachers would have no students and therefore no jobs.

Parents should watch the actual curriculum of a career program carefully, no matter what progressive name is put on new programs. Although a program may carry the title of "Industrial Technology," "Marketing Management," or "Institutional Diatetics," check the actual course work. What percentage of the curriculum is loaded with the same old obsolete courses created just after World War I? Many high schools and public junior colleges wrap up the same old garbage in a fancy wrapper and bilk the ignorant students into taking it and bilk the ignorant public into paying for it.

The curriculum for many career programs is built around the needs of the institution, not the needs of the student or the demands of the career. The institution has faculty members whose own training is obsolete but who must be employed. And of course, since these faculty members are the persons who design the new career programs, they all make very sure their jobs are protected. Johnnie loses, you lose, and society loses.

This problem falls under the jurisdiction of the curriculum director, the superintendent, and the board of education. This is a bigger problem than can be handled at the neighborhood school level. You should get something done about the policy concerning the curriculum of career programs. This would take group parental action. If parents were to organize a task-group for this problem, they should be sure to include in the group professional members of some of the career under consideration. As career programs are revised for relevancy, these people can speak to the board, which decides policy, with greater authority and expertise than any of the educators.

On an individual basis, since Johnnie is interested in a career program now, you could check out the specific course requirements to weed out the obsolete ones. Demand that Johnnie be admitted to the valuable parts of the program without having to take the courses which have no value. In their place he can choose other courses which you and he deem more valuable for him. You'll get some static on this because the designers of these programs have built in the rule that students must take the whole package or nothing at all. This, of course, is designed to preserve the sacred cows of vocational education. Apply Parental Persistence to get what you want for Johnnie.

We know one young man who enrolled in a public junior-college program in automechanics. The applied part of the program was excellent, and the young man excelled. But he was required to take several sacred-cow courses, including "Basic Math." He was an intelligent man who was finally expelled from the program because he refused to attend the basic math class. This young man, who had studied high school mathematics through trigonometry successfully, was forced to spend ten hours a week doing what he considered third-grade arithmetic. Society lost a good automechanic because of educators' inflexibility or stupidity. Why was he not excused from that particular portion of the program which he did not need? He was told that if exceptions were made, there would be a rash of requests from other students. This could have meant only that the needs of the institution were more important than those of the students.

4

"Gotcha" Games

"Gotcha" games are what the schools play when the staff doesn't know how to handle a child. Out of their own frustration, the school staff "does a number" on your child to "protect" itself. By "protect," we mean the protection of the staff's jobs. "Gotcha" games are never in the interest of the child; they are games created, played, and refereed by the school personnel only. The opposition, you and your child, never get a chance to play until the last quarter of the game after the school staff has rigged the game with a score of 90-0. The only reason you get to play during the last quarter is that the school system entitles this quarter "public relations." They must at least inform the opponent that he was officially in the game so that he can accept the results of the game.

The goal of "Gotcha" games is always the same. It's called "getting rid of Johnnie." There are many variations of the game, but if you are prepared for it and know what to look for, you can easily recognize that the school's decision always means that the school will no longer attempt to educate Johnnie. Johnnie has become an embarassment to them, and they must desensitize him, either directly or indirectly, so that the teachers can continue to do their "oatmeal" act, the highly repetitive, only act they know, unthinkingly and imperturbably. Your Johnnie is interfering with that act.

Some of these games are subtle at first and some not so subtle. You often don't know you've even been playing until you've lost the game. Johnnie and you have been "handled" right out of Johnnie's educational rights. But there are things you can do if you learn to recognize the signals that a game is going on. Although you haven't been told that you are a player, the school team cannot play the game without signals. You must learn to recognize the signals and begin playing before they want you to play. The earlier you begin playing, the better your chances, as in any game.

"Build a Case" (Trouble Begins)

The first "Gotcha" game is a subtle, early-stage game, and many parents don't recognize the game. Even if they do realize that things are not exactly "right," they haven't anything tangible enough to get concerned about. Parents will get signals that this game is in its early stages from things Johnnie brings home, things he is puzzled about.

If Johnnie begins to tell you that he is being singled out to be punished for little things that most of the other kids do all the time with little more than mild admonishments from the school staff, this is a signal. Johnnie will perceive that the school personnel are watching him very closely and treating every small infraction as though it were a federal case. It generally takes Johnnie a couple of weeks or more to realize the difference between the way he is being handled and the way the other kids are being handled for the same actions.

Other signals might appear, such as casual comments by teachers to Johnnie. Some of the school personnel aren't as good players as others, and those not-so-apt players sometimes reveal signals to Johnnie, signals that are supposed to be verbalized only among the faculty. Johnnie might be told, "We're watching you," or "We've got your number." The really bad players might even reveal more by saying such things as, "Ms. Soinso told me about you," or "Mr. Soinso has warned us all to make sure you toe the mark."

When you start getting feedback from Johnnie along these lines, don't pass it off as unimportant. If you do, not only is Johnnie going to be miserable and have a difficult time learning under these conditions, but also, sooner or later, something is going to erupt as a major problem, probably Johnnie. You should act before the "Build a Case" game goes very far and you are involved in a tougher game. If Johnnie erupts in reaction to the discriminatory treatment, then his eruption is a tangible fact to be used against him later. That is part of the goal of "Build a Case."

Just as soon as you are alert to the signals, you should get into the game and begin building Johnnie's case also. The thing not to do here is to talk with any of the school people; if you do, they'll simply unload on you the case they have built, and you have accepted the defensive side for Johnnie. Remember that Johnnie is entitled to and needs his side represented since there are always two teams to every game, as there are two sides to every conflict. And you are the only person on Johnnie's team. You need to take the offensive.

You should find out what is going on. Don't verbally express any concern; don't have a discussion with the teachers. Just sit in on the classes your Johnnie is in and observe. Be polite and pleasant, but observe the teachers Johnnie has. Take a note pad with you and take notes on what kind of teacher-behavior you observe. Even if you don't consider anything important enough to write down, write something in your notebook for effect. Rattle the teachers' cages the way they have been rattling Johnnie's.

Observe not only how the teachers treat Johnnie but also how they treat the other kids. You need to observe "differences" in the way the teachers treat the kids. You might want to alert some other parents whose offspring you suspect might not be getting a fair deal. You will be, in essence, watching the school personnel in the same eagle-eyed fashion that they are watching Johnnie. Your "notes" on your teacher-observations can be as objective as you want to make them, and certainly they will be as objective as the observations of the teachers when they make their reports of Johnnie.

As you observe the teachers, see if you can single out the problem-teachers who might have initiated the case against Johnnie. If you recognize a teacher as one who seems insecure and/or having a difficult time of it with many of the children, you might have pegged the instigator. Visit that teacher's class frequently, even at times of the day when your Johnnie is not with her.

List in your notebook every kind of inappropriate teacher-behavior you can find. Don't be afraid to make a long list. You might need it. Nobody needs to see this except you, and it is your tool in case you need it.

No doubt, someone, probably a teacher, will attempt to talk with you. The teachers will be curious about your presence, and perhaps feel threatened. Since the school has so far made no overt or open charges to you about Johnnie, you should also observe the rules of this particular game.

> Ms. WHATCHADOING: It's nice that you could come to visit us. We're always happy to see parents. [That's a barefaced lie, and the opening; now you are supposed to reveal your purpose. Don't.]

> YOU: Yes, we are always interested in what is going on at school. We want Johnnie to have every opportunity for the best education possible. [Po-

lite, but you've hinted that the school is under inspection, not Johnnie's behavior.]

MS. WHATCHADOING: Yes, well, we think we have a very good program here, one of the best in the area. We have a good team of teachers who are doing a very good job. [She's revealed a defensiveness, and she is stating in the positive that there is evidently some concern that someone might criticize. She is also trying to get you to agree with her and to trust the school personnel so that the game will be easier. In order to get the school staff members off of Johnnie's back, you need to intimidate them a bit.]

YOU: Yes, I'm sure you feel that way, but a good program can be interpreted many different ways, needs monitoring, and can always be improved. [You didn't criticize them, but you didn't reassure them either.]

MS. WHATCHADOING: [Uncomfortable because your lines were not what is expected from manipulated parents.] Yes, of course. You know, if only Johnnie were a little more interested in school. Did you notice how inattentive he was during social studies? [You're supposed to feel defensive now and apologetic for Johnnie. The conversation has shifted away from scrutiny of the school to scrutiny of Johnnie.]

YOU: Yes, that is strange. Johnnie has always been interested in social studies in the past. It is odd that he has become so turned-off here. [Shame on you for not being cooperative with her. She probably will decide at this point that she doesn't know how to deal with you, because you are not performing the way parents are supposed to perform.]

Ms. WHATCHADOING: Yes, well, I must get out on the playground now. Come and visit us anytime. [Playground nothing—she wants to get away from you, and she's probably going to the faculty coffee room and talk about how "odd" you are.]

Your very presence and record-keeping may be all that is needed to inform the school personnel that maybe they better call the game a tie, because you will not let them win unopposed. Any one of the school players might end up a casualty in the game if it goes on. If this action does not end the game, you'll be better prepared for the next game, a more serious game. You at least know the other players, the playing field, and what kind of players are in the game, their style, their tactics, and possibly their weaknesses.

"Sidetrack"

When Oatmeal doesn't work, many school people are thrown into confusion. They don't know what to do with the child; he often begins to misbehave and give them a bad time. At this point, in self-defense, they might begin to play "Build a Case," but after assessing the parents or after being foiled in "Build a Case," the more devious school people often resort to the game of "Sidetrack," which is becoming increasingly popular. It involves removing Johnnie from the Oatmeal learning situation and *wasting* his time doing "something else." Parents should not be too quick to label a switch as "Sidetrack," because in ideal individualized instruction, Johnnie should be given alternate instruction when Oatmeal doesn't work. But you want to look very closely at what they are having Johnnie do as an alternative and how he is spending his time. In "Sidetrack," Johnnie will be *wasting* his time in a multitude of ways, all of which are designed to do two things, keep Johnnie busy and keep him out of the teachers' hair.

Sidetrack is a difficult game to recognize, and by the time parents recognize it, the game has often been won by the school and the damage has been done to the child. This game is usually played best in open-space schools and in individualized programs. Although these two educational innovations have much merit when properly used, they do lend themselves beautifully to Sidetrack. In these settings the sidetracking is generally not noticed by the student or the parents for a long time. It is often a year or two before the parents know that their child has been had, and he has lost a year or two of learning.

The first clue that Sidetrack is beginning is your learning from Johnnie that he has been shifted to activities that most of the other kids are not doing. You have to be in the habit of frequently discussing Johnnie's schoolwork with him to recognize a shift. You should find out very quickly just what he is doing. Common sidetracks are: having Johnnie repeat programmed materials he did months or even years ago; having Johnnie complete endless, unrelated, mimeographed materials the teachers have pulled from their files at random to keep him busy; physically removing Johnnie from a regular skill class and assigning him busywork without benefit of any instruction; giving him "busywork" that is so easy for him that it makes no demands on him or the teacher, allowing him to spend essential-skills time playing games that are generally reserved as rewards or enrichment tools for the children in the mainstream, for example, checkers or chess. This last is insidious because Johnnie is more than happy to be released from challenging academic work and allowed to play games. But you won't be so happy two or three years from now when you find out that Johnnie has slipped two or three years of reading, mathematics, language skills, or whatever. The next school might not be so easy on Johnnie.

If you sense that the school might be playing Sidetrack with Johnnie, have Johnnie explain to you what he is doing; if he cannot explain it to you, then you have a possible clue. Ask Johnnie how much help he is getting from the teachers. Have him bring some of the work home for you to see and to appraise. If you are still suspicious, tackle the teacher or teachers in charge of the particular academic subjects in which you suspect he has been sidetracked.

Find out from the teachers what their specific objectives are. Have them explain their planned, sequenced program (related materials building toward a goal). Ask to see the materials they are using, the materials they plan to use in future weeks and months. You appraise the material if they produce some. Is the material sequenced; does the material fit together? Where does it lead? Where will it put Johnnie academically, compared to the other children?

If Johnnie needs alternative learning methods, and the school has designed an appropriate one, you'll get good answers to these questions. If Johnnie has been sidetracked, you'll know it. The teachers won't have good answers to these questions because they are simply allowing him to slip further and further behind the mainstream because it is easier for them. They've quit on Johnnie, and they are occupying him with busywork.

Should you not get satisfactory answers, state firmly that you expect the school to teach Johnnie the skills he needs and that you won't allow the teachers to allow Johnnie to waste his time in their school. Tell them that you require from them a well-conceived program based on objective assessment of Johnnie's needs. Give them some time, a couple of weeks or so, to produce these things, but not too much time because Johnnie is wasting his time while they create a program.

If and when they produce what you ask, require an explanation of the assessment tools; view the results yourself; look at the whole of the planned program materials they anticipate using. Ask for literature or other proof that explains where Johnnie will be in grade-level equivalents after completion of the program. Ask to see research results which prove the worth of the materials. If you suspect the staff of avoiding the point, insist that they put the program plan in writing for you.

Don't let the educators bamboozle you with the school jargon, and don't let them try to impress you with vagaries. If you don't understand the terms they use, or the materials, ask questions. Remember always, that these materials are designed for your child to understand. Someone on the school "team" should have the expertise to interpret the program to your satisfaction. Don't be embarrassed into backing off. A good salesman has to be able to explain his product to the buyer if he wants a sale. Remember, you are the buyer, and your child is the consumer.

A Sidetrack Conference

YOU: I don't understand why Johnnie has been removed from his math class, and I want to know just what he is doing now. I want you to explain it all to me.

Ms. DERAILER: Johnnie was just not getting anything out of the regular math class, not paying attention, causing commotion, disturbing the other kids [she is expressing *her* needs, not Johnnie's], and so I decided to move him into the conference room and let him work alone.

YOU: I see. Now what is he doing?

Ms. DERAILER: I'm having him work on exercises that he is weak in.

YOU: Would you show me the exercises he has been doing?

Ms. DERAILER: Certainly. [She goes to file cabinet

and begins pulling out mimeographed sheets for you to see.]

YOU: Now the regular class was working on long division [or binomial equations, etc.]. Are they using these same materials?

MS. DERAILER: Well, yes, I use these exercises as supplemental exercises for some of the students.

YOU: You said these are supplemental exercises. What is Johnnie now using for a main sequenced program?

MS. DERAILER: Johnnie is not ready for further work yet, so I'm having him drill on these exercises.

YOU: How long are you going to have him do this "drill"? And what sequenced approach have you planned for him?

MS. DERAILER: Well, I haven't gone that far yet. I suppose he will use the regular book the others are using. [She just put her foot in her mouth. She has no plan for Johnnie, and if he moves ahead with the regular book he will do it without benefit of the teacher-instruction which the main group is getting. Evidently, the philosophy is that if a child cannot understand the material with teacher-instruction, let him learn it on his own.]

YOU: You have no objectives for Johnnie, no sequenced plan for his independent study, and you are denying him any instruction. For a boy who is having difficulty with math, how do you expect him to learn under those conditions?

MS. DERAILER: I'll help him, by giving him instruction as he needs it.

YOU: That won't do. You have physically isolated

him so that he cannot get help during class time because you are busy with the regular class. You've made no provision to give him individual instruction any other part of the day, and you have not even thought out a well-conceived program for self-instruction. If you insist that he remain isolated from the regular class, then I insist that you develop a sequenced plan for his math education and make provision for help from you when you are not busy with another class. [You have in essence given her another "class" to prepare each day.]

MS. DERAILER: That's impossible. I don't have that kind of time and the way he acts up in class, I won't have him in my class.

YOU: You do not have the authority to make that kind of decision to deprive a child of his educational rights.

MS. DERAILER: [Angry now.] You mean you condone his disrupting my class?

YOU: No, I do not. But your action has no regard for the child; it is too drastic and too permanent. [She's done nothing but try to make her job easier.] I insist that you teach math to Johnnie. I don't care if it is in the conference room or in the regular classroom, but I will not have him permanently deprived of math instruction.

MS. DERAILER: Well, if he can behave, he can come back to the regular group. [She is compromising, taking the second easiest course of action since you've foiled the easiest route for her.]

YOU: I'll speak to Johnnie and insist that he improve his behavior, but I expect you to work with him to help him catch up with the rest of the group for the time you've had him in isolation.

Ms. Derailer will not be happy with Johnnie or you, and Johnnie will probably not get the best kind of math instruction he needs, but at least the teacher's "regular" instruction is available to him. He will not be relegated to some corner doing busywork with no instruction. A child often misbehaves in class as a defense mechanism when he doesn't understand the classwork. A child who feels adequate and feels he is accomplishing something rarely misbehaves in class.

"You can't play"

This is the discriminatory exclusion of a student from participation in a school activity—on a permanent basis. The wrestling coach, baseball coach, or choir director says, "I won't have that kid on my team [in my choir, etc.]."

To permanently revoke a student's privilege to participate in an extracurricular activity is downright stupidity on the part of the educator who is responsible. If the school has a motivation or behavior problem with this student, the school should use this activity constructively as a motivator. The school staff should work out a contract arrangement with the student whereby he earns the right to participate in his chosen activity for specified periods of good behavior. By permanently revoking this privilege, the school staff is destroying the only reason many kids have for even being in school, especially kids with school problems.

Exclusion is poor psychology and the educators are breeding dropout attitudes. If the excluded student does not drop out of school, the staff has defeated not only the child but also itself and can expect nothing but misbehavior from this student. Educators who permanently exclude students from activities are not meeting the needs of the kids they are supposed to be serving, and ultimately they are not meeting the needs of society. Therefore, you are going to have to do something about this kind of poor judgment.

You-Can't-Play Conference

At this conference, as with any conference to correct faulty teacher decisions, it is wise to include personnel other than the particular person responsible for the improper action. Include the principal, perhaps the counselor in your conference with Mr. Excluder. They can exert pressure to change *his* mind.

> YOU: You have kicked Suzie out of choir for the rest of the year. You should know that choir is the only thing that Suzie likes about school. She has an excellent voice, likes to sing, and it is the only lever we've had for supporting the school to her. Your action robs Suzie of her only reason for going to school. I want you to work out a way for her to return to the choir.

> MR. EXCLUDER: Mrs. Parent, I can't put up with Suzie's behavior in my choir. She is ruining it. She talks all the time, chews gum, shows up late frequently. We are preparing for state competition, and she is an obstacle.

> YOU: The purpose of choir and every other activity here is to help students develop their abilities and interests and to find their place in our society. The choir exists for the needs of the kids, not for your gratification.

> MR. EXCLUDER: Mrs. Parent, I must have some standards. If I put up with Suzie's behavior, I will have chaos. My choir is one of the finest in the state. We wouldn't have a choir if we permitted the students to behave just as they please. [Notice how he keeps saying "my" choir.]

YOU: I understand what you are saying. Of course, you must have some standards, and I don't condone improper behavior from Suzie. I am saying that your action is too drastic, too permanent. You are working with young adolescents, not a professional group; your first responsibility is to the children as an educator.

MR. EXCLUDER: When I kicked her out last Wednesday, I had had it. She had kept the soprano section in an uproar all week. I tried to ignore it, but there is a limit . . .

YOU: Of course there is a limit. But you need to define those limits to the kids, not ignore the problems. Suzie says she wasn't aware that she was behaving badly enough to be kicked out.

MR. PRINCIPAL: Perhaps you could work out an agreement with Suzie, Mr. Excluder, so that she understands the consequences of improper behavior. If she enjoys choir, a short suspension might be adequate to enforce proper behavior. [He is seeking a compromise.]

YOU: I think that would be a good idea.

MR. EXCLUDER: If she can behave, of course I'd like to have her voice in my choir. Have her come in and see me.

When using an activity privilege as a motivating lever to encourage academic application or behavior control, the school staff must be very careful not to make the standards so high, especially at first, that there is no chance for the student to be successful in earning the privilege. Educators often forget that goals must be kept within the reach of the student, within the realm of possibility. Too often, educators set perfection standards for problem kids; therefore, they have doomed the kid to failure.

You may have to remind the school that "improvement" is the goal of the school for each individual student. A kid having a tough time of it academically or behaviorally should be made to feel successful and rewarded for the improvement he does make, even though it is not at the perfection level. No one, not even teachers, always operates at perfection level. How long would these educators continue on the job if they forfeited a full year's salary if they deviated from perfection only once?

Unfortunately, some althletic coaches, drama coaches, music directors, and club sponsors do not always have the best interests of the kids at heart. Too many coaches have their own needs in mind. Many kids are sacrificed so that the coach or sponsor can have a celebrated reputation for producing the best team, the best choir, the best Future Homemakers' project, or whatever. The goal of some of these educators is to achieve personal, national recognition in their fields. The real purpose of extracurricular activities is not to achieve professional advancement for teachers; it is to motivate and educate young people. Glory-seeking activity sponsors are often guilty of refusing to have a problem kid in their activity. Such refusal is a dereliction of duty.

Typical of this attitude and behavior is one elementary science teacher who treated the children deprecatingly, and considered them trespassers in her room full of science materials. The kids thoroughly hated her because of her bad disposition. She fenced off a large section of the already-too-small playground to plant a tree farm. She wrote up her ecology project and proclaimed her superiority. This hated teacher was declared a "Teacher of the Year" in her state for her "progressive" ecology project.

Label/Libel—The Problem Conference

The problem conference is the usual setting for the presentation to you of a derogatory label for your Johnnie. You will be invited to school with saccharine politeness for the problem conference because of the school's "very deep concern" for the child. Don't believe it. Their very deep concern is often for themselves. The problem conference is often the occasion for the announcement to you that the label/libel game has been played; and the heart of that game is that the school offers you only labels, not solutions. When the school plays this game, it has quit on Johnnie and is throwing the problem into your lap.

If the school can succeed in assigning your child a derogatory label, and they can succeed in making that label stick, that label excuses any punishment or scapegoatism the school personnel want to use. After the label is affixed, the school's goal is to "control" the child only; their educational responsibility is to "the other children." Somehow, the educational profession has firmly entrenched in it the philosophy that the act of attaching a label ends the school's responsibility; educators attach labels without compunction. Their conscience is at ease after the label is decided. They have been automatically excused from educating the child.

What kind of labels do they use? The labels run the gamut, but they are all bad; pugnacious, hostile, aggressive, immature, obnoxious, stubborn, lazy, uncooperative, disturbed, emotionally disturbed—are just a few. This name-calling does not do anything to help the child; they are defensive names used to protect the school from criticism. Actually, all of these labels indicate that since the school is evoking bad behavior from Johnnie, something is wrong with the way they are handling him.

But isn't it true that many kids do exhibit these

traits? Certainly, everyone does, even teachers at times, within limits. By dishing out these labels to parents in a conference, the school is saying that the child is "impossible" for them. A school which really does have deep concern for a child with problems, will take any personality traits into consideration and plan positive, appropriate approaches for not only controlling the child but also changing the need for the bad behavior and educating the child also. Children who exhibit bad behavior are expressing some unmet need, some inadequacy, or are retaliating for someone else's bad behavior, possibly the teacher's.

In the label conference, the school team will confront you with all the evidence they have that there is something wrong with Johnnie, implying that there is something wrong with the way you have raised him. They will present you with their labels and suggest, ever so politely and solicitously, that Johnnie should see a psychologist or that he needs "child guidance," another polite way of labeling a child. When this kind of suggestion is made, you as parents should not try to deal with the suggestion immediately. You should remember that these teachers do not have the training to make psychological diagnoses, and even if they were correct, your first problem is to deal with Johnnie's schooling. You need to find out what is behind what they are saying, and you should immediately be suspicious enough to find out what the school might be concealing, what kinds of errors it is making. Perhaps the school has a deranged teacher on the staff who should see a psychologist.

If parents suspect that the school has been playing "Gotcha" games, parents should never go into a school conference without the impartial witness, the tape recorder. A simple, inexpensive cassette with a built-in microphone does fine for this. It is your right to have a record of the conference. You can be sure that the principal will write an extremely biased account of what transpired at the conference, including an on-the-spot psychological diagnosis of you during the conference. Sometimes school records explain away all of Johnnie's school problems on the basis of the principal's amateur psychological diagnosis of Johnnie and you.

Really, isn't this rather paranoid? Yes, it is. But we are living in a paranoid society, and the school people are among the most paranoid when it comes to parents. In self-defense, educators frequently use the label conference for the purpose of inducing confusion and guilt in the parents. If the parents can be made to feel confused and guilty enough, they are not likely to question the school or criticize it.

A favorite school tactic for handling problem conferences is to intimidate parents by confronting them with the whole team of professionals. This team has probably already had the real conference earlier at which all the decisions were made—all the decisions for manipulating the parents. By using the "team" approach to the conference, having seven or ten persons facing you when you walk into the conference room, the school has put you into an uncomfortable position, tending to intimidate you. This is a favorite tactic of insecure educators who are trying "to do a number" on your child. If you have your tape recorder there, you will intimidate them also, and you will have something closer to approximating equality of representation.

But aren't educators basically honest? Not necessarily. They must protect their jobs at all cost; sad though it is, many educators operate out of expediency. You have to keep them honest. The major reason parents should tape-record problem conferences is to prevent school people from telling you three different, conflicting stories within the same half-hour conference. If you are involved in a situation at the label-libel level, it is very possible you

may have future problems and future conferences. The
impartial, unbiased tape gathers contradictory statements, statements often made by the same person who
would later deny having said them.

School people make mistakes sometimes, slip and say
things that do not support the "team goal." Sometimes,
minor members of the team are not privy to the team goal
and could be your child's advocate on tape even though
they have no intention of doing so. When you get contradictions and conflicting statements, you may want to pin
down the persons responsible, which you cannot do without a tape if those persons deny having made those statements. When unscrupulous educators resort to these con-
fusing, switch-story tactics and succeed in handling you,
you need facts for disarming them. The tape is also good
for catching innuendoes, incongruities and clues to the
school's next step or next game if they win this one.

What about what I say? One of the main things which
should be uppermost in your mind during the problem conference is that you must be totally the defender of the
child; no matter what kind of problems you might be
coping with at home, don't be candid. The school does not
need any more script-fuel to use against Johnnie. You
must deal with any problems you have at home alone; the
school cannot be of any help in the home situation and you
don't need their condescending advice. The home does not
concern them. But the school situation does concern you
and could be the reason for any problems you might be
having with Johnnie. A child who is mishandled all day,
experiencing harassment and frustration, cannot help but
bring some of this home. Don't look to the school for any
help with your home problems or for any sympathy. If
you do, your confidence will probably be used against
Johnnie. Two parents should defer their personal discussion about Johnnie until they are home. And don't give

the school people any sympathy because it will be interpreted by them to be affirmation of their label-diagnosis
and their mismanagement.

FATAL DECISION
WHEELING, ILLINOIS
Des Moines Register, December 25, 1975 (AP)
Eleven-year-old Montgomery Klemmer excused him-
self while his parents talked with a counselor at
Wheeling High School, and when his mother went to
look for him a half hour later, she found him hanged
from a towel in a dispenser in the school washroom.

If you accept the label, then you have given the
school permission to do nothing constructive. One of the
goals of the label-libel game is to throw you off balance
so that you will not question the school people about their
responsibilities. You will not ask about your child's learning or what the school is doing to ameliorate the problems. Their hope is that you will be so shot-down and
confused by the labels they are throwing around that you
won't question them on their misbehavior and responsibility. They are saying that they don't have to deal with
the problem; they have thrown the ball into your lap; and
that ball is a medicine ball.

But you, of course, are looking for solutions, and they
are not helping you. If the schools were operating on a
free-enterprise basis, or on the voucher system, at this
point you would withdraw Johnnie from that school. But
our monopolistic school systems are protected from loss
of customers, no matter how badly the educators behave,
by compulsory attendance laws in all fifty states. The
voucher system, an emerging parent-option in some places,
is discussed elsewhere in this volume.

What should I do? The best approach for parents at
the problem conference is to let the tape recorder run and
listen to what the school people have to say. Be non-
committal, don't react, don't be frightened, or intimidated.

And don't leave the conference confused, and whipped, feeling as though you've just been told that Johnnie has terminal cancer.

After the school staff has heaped you with all the dung-like labels, and has thrown you the medicine ball, you throw it right back in their laps where it belongs:

> YOU: We're only parents. You are educators. What are your suggestions for dealing with the problems you have? [Make sure you say *"your* problems," not "our problems" or "Johnnie's problems." Don't be on their team.] What solutions have you thought about? What solutions have you checked into? What alternatives are you prepared to discuss with us for our approval? [Probably at this point, you'll have "got" them, because all they were prepared to do was to unload their problem on you with a label.]

> "TEAM" LEADER: We feel that Johnnie has psychological problems, and we're just classroom teachers and not prepared to handle that. We feel that before anything can be done for Johnnie, we must get to the root of the problem. [He has dumped it into your lap with a label. It is ironic that as educators they claim not to be prepared to educate a problem child but they evidently feel they are qualified to diagnose and label him psychologically. Don't let them get away with it; don't let them "off the hook."]

> YOU: Many children may have "psychological" problems, and probably many teachers do also, but we want you to deal in specifics with Johnnie's education, not in the vagaries of pseudopsychology. I expect you to deal in educational problems. Attaching a label to Johnnie does not excuse you from teaching him his arithmetic and reading [or what-

ever subject matter is appropriate]. I want you to expend some effort to design a well-conceived program to educate Johnnie. When you have done this, we'll talk again.

THEM: But we are just not equipped to deal in these problems. [They are appealing to you for sympathy and confirmation. Don't give it to them.]

YOU: I understand that, and I respect you for acknowledging your limitations, but I do not approve of your quitting on Johnnie's education. There are federal programs, state programs, county programs, area programs, multitudinous tax-paid consultants, and directors at every level for dealing with school inadequacies. I want you to get the help you need to know how to teach Johnnie his arithmetic and reading [or whatever]. I want you to consider all of this carefully and seriously and to present your plans to me for my approval. I expect you to present several alternatives for handling your deficiencies in educating Johnnie. [You've thrown the medicine ball back in their laps where it belongs, but you've also reserved for yourself the final decision.]

What options are they likely to offer? There are a couple of solutions that the school might offer that you should be prepared to refuse categorically. The school will very likely suggest that Johnnie see the school psychologist. Don't agree to it. Rather, ask for alternative educational measures for handling the problem. If the educational staff is qualified to make bar-stool psychological diagnoses, then it certainly should be equipped to plan educationally for this child. A psychological diagnosis hasn't much to do with educational management of the child, and the staff needs to deal at that level, no matter what a psychologist might say. The chapter entitled "Hot

Air Balloons" suggests that in some cases parents not use school psychologists but that they should obtain the services of a psychologist in private practice for an impartial diagnosis, one that does not reflect the "team" goal.

If you decide not to use the school psychologist, then insist that the school deal with the educational problems only. Let the *educators* consult the school psychologist, or a learning consultant to help them to know what to do. Many school psychologists attach labels and confirm teacher-diagnoses only—without helping the child. That kind of school psychologist Johnnie does not need.

Another solution that might be offered is that of sending Johnnie to a residential school for "problem" kids that is located somewhere in the area. This is tantamount to sending Johnnie to reform school because these schools are the dumping ground for all the public schools' failures. Permitting a child to be sent to one of these schools attaches an indelible label to the child that cannot easily be removed. That label may haunt the child for the rest of his life. And it is so unnecessary.

Whether the name is "Happy House" or "New Start Horizons," these institutions do little more than stigmatize your child. Most of these institutions are staffed by sociologists with very little training, who often do not have credentials in psychology or education, let alone psychiatry. Yet these sociologists will diagnose Johnnie's problems and attempt to educate him in the same academics the professionally trained school staff failed to do. Residential schools of this type are primarily for children who do not have concerned parents to protect them.

Should you be having problems with Johnnie at home and cannot cope with him and feel the school has just reason for its opinion, then we refer you to the chapter on special education. Remember that the public schools have access to trained professionals with much better qualifications for educating Johnnie than most last-resort residential schools—if serious problems really do exist.

But *you* should make that decision and *you* should determine the appropriate course of action. In the meantime, make sure Johnnie does not receive a psychological label he does not deserve from unqualified persons who are looking for an excuse for their own inadequacies.

What if the school does not offer any other solutions? If this happens, then use Parental Persistence to insist that the staff design alternative solutions. Notice the plural. Ask for several plans, not just one. Insist that a time limit be set for presentation of these plans and agree on a date for your next conference to discuss the plans.

And if they do? Listen to the plans and let your tape recorder run. Don't commit yourself. Go home, play it back through again, and then make your decision at home in private. You need a chance to sort through all the garbage on the tape, and you need privacy to discuss your personal feelings, and you need time to consider a decision as important as this one.

If the school presents only one solution and it does not seem to you to be a very good solution, tell the school staff that you don't consider it a very good solution and that you think they should consider the matter further and come up with some other possibilities. Tell them that you don't consider the plan they presented to be the best they can do, that it is not representative of their best work. You can be sure they have said the same to your child.

Kangaroo Court

One of the things parents should attempt to discover in any problem conference is whether or not every one of the individual teachers and other staff members is in total agreement with the libelous label just tied to Johnnie. If no one has anything good to say about the child, and the staff is in 100-percent agreement, then something is

wrong with that staff. Either the staff members are terribly inadequate, unimaginative and negative, or they are
terribly threatened into agreement by their superiors. If
there is nothing positive to be said for Johnnie in this
conference, then you are probably dealing with a very
rotten barrel of apples.

Truly professional educators know that they cannot
completely understand any child, and the true professional
knows she is "practicing," just as the medical doctor
"practices." There are not many proof-positive diagnoses.
Medical doctors often try many different medications for
problem ailments, and different doctors believe in and
will use different treatments to obtain results. The same
should be true of educators, but often individual educators
are thwarted in trying to save the child because their
superiors or "team" demand 100-percent agreement to
avoid criticism.

In self-protection, the school staff has banded together *against* the child. This kind of mob-psychology is
largely responsible for the feeble advancements made in
education over the years. Medical doctors would still be
bloodletting and using leeches if this same philosophy had
been practiced in the medical profession. Good educators
shudder every time they hear an administrator insist that
the staff be in 100-percent agreement. Be forewarned:
When you catch even echoes of this kind of unanimous
certainty, the conference will be nothing but a kangaroo
court.

*What if the school staff all agree and I don't accept
it?* If you accept their diagnosis, the school has excused
itself from responsibility, and they hope they have loaded
you with guilt. This is a no-win situation for the child—
if you let the label stick.

YOU: We've listened to everything you have said
and understand what you are saying. Everything
you've said is negative condemnation of Johnnie.

I find it strange that no one here has anything good to say about Johnnie, and no one here has any positive suggestions which show any understanding of our son or concern for him.

TEAM LEADER: Oh, but Ms. Parent, we feel very sorry for Johnnie, and the whole staff has done everything it can to help him. We feel now that he needs help beyond our expertise.

YOU: Probably you do need help, but something is wrong when this many persons all agree and yet have no helpful suggestions. I do not accept this blanket condemnation of my child. If none of you has any positive suggestions or any insight into my child's problems, then something is wrong with this school and the employment policies of the district.

TEAM LEADER: But Ms. Parent, taking that attitude is not going to help your child. [This is a threat.] We are all trying to help Johnnie.

YOU: Then you offer some positive suggestions. I want you to individually list those things that are "good" about Johnnie, his strengths, with the purpose of viewing him positively enough for you to discover a way to help him. [They won't be happy with you for this, but you've put them "on." You haven't accepted their unanimity.] Now, I want each one of you to consider what you, individually, could do to help him. And I'm going to talk with each of you individually during this next week to learn what each of you has come up with. I want you to be creative.

Will this work? Maybe. By insisting on dealing with each of them individually and charging them with a task, you have shown that you will not accept the kangaroo-court approach or the label dispensed by it. And you might be freeing up a couple good teachers to do what they would like to do to help Johnnie. Sometimes if the school staff knows that you will not allow them to play their game, they will call off the game.

"Grill the child" This is probably the most vicious game a school can play. The school's aim in this game, in the interim between the problem conference and the actual professional psychological diagnosis, is to rattle the kid so that he does test poorly and manifest the traits the teachers have attributed to him. They are trying to create behaviors which support their opinion. They must prove their point if you should reject their psychological diagnosis.

In this game, a group of teachers, two, three, or more, get the child cornered and privately give him "the third degree," using the worst sort of tactics that have been condemned as "police brutality" in recent years. Police harassment of criminals is not permitted in America today, yet teachers sometimes practice the worst sort of brainwashing on your children. It is ironic that our society protects criminals from this abuse and yet allows it to be practiced on its children.

A young child is very vulnerable to this sort of harassment. The young child who is grilled can become so rattled, so confused, that he begins to question his own perceptions. And that is exactly what the school is after in "Grill the child," especially if the child has reported experiencing improper or illegal behavior from the staff. They are using the child to cover their tracks. If you, a secure adult, were to experience three or four persons, let alone your superiors, telling you that you didn't see what you saw, even you could become dubious about your own perceptions. Brainwashing tactics work very well with adults, and they work even better with children who have, in a good home situation, cultivated a certain respect for adult authority.

Can this be dealt with? Yes, but it means discrediting the teachers to the child. Tell Johnnie that he is not to talk with more than one teacher at a time unless at least one of his parents is present. Instruct him to say he cannot discuss any school problems aside from academics without his parents.

Isn't this a lot of responsibility to place on a child? Yes, it is; but it must be done sometimes to protect the child, and older children, especially, can handle it. The other method of coping with this sort of extreme mental cruelty is to simply keep the child home from school until some solution is reached. This might seem drastic to some parents, but they must remember that their child's mental health is at stake. Ask yourself how many days you would stay on a job which you completely detested and during which days you were browbeaten all day long. There are many teachers out there whose job security is more important to them than your child's mental health.

How can Johnnie learn if I keep him out of school? Your child will not be losing any learning because he can't be learning anything in this sort of environment; he'll be losing only harassment by staying out of school. The only thing he could learn in school in this sort of situation is hate, hostility, and aggression which would be unleashed in a safer setting, very likely at home. If you leave a child in a situation this bad, he is very likely to develop emotional problems.

"Grill the child" sometimes deteriorates even further when a teacher is emotionally disturbed or is merely a vindictive person used to having her own way. This sort of teacher may turn other children against Johnnie by her own modeling. Children imitate authority; and if they witness a teacher persecuting Johnnie, they assume (learn) that Johnnie is to be persecuted. If he becomes the object of peer-derision or peer-abuse, then you better get him out of that situation immediately. Children who have been taught this kind of scapegoatism by a disturbed teacher will soon find another scapegoat. Even if your child isn't the object of this extreme cruelty, he is suffering at the hands of this teaching. Society will suffer as long as this kind of teacher is allowed to work.

Parent Punisher

What does a "suspension" mean, and what can be done about it? A suspension, whether it is for two days or two weeks, means that the school people need a rest and have declared themselves a vacation from trying to cope with Johnnie. They really don't know how to handle the situation, so they have declared "time out" so that they don't have to cope with it for a while. And they don't even mentally cope with the problem during this time. What ideally should be a cooling off time, so that the school could devise a positive plan for handling its problems, becomes the end in itself. The respite period turns into a spite period.

Suspension is viewed by the school as a parent punishment, in this case actually physically throwing the problem into the parents' hands. It is the school's lever for forcing the parents to "do something;" generally, it is the school's means for forcing the parents to go along with and enforce the school's punishment system for handling Johnnie.

The school's philosophy is that some parents will not react, will not pay attention, to the problems the staff is having with Johnnie until the school throws Johnnie out into the streets, which is what suspension does. The real intention behind suspension is that the school considers Johnnie so terrible that they send him home to stay as a punishment to the parents for raising such a monster.

Suspension "for cause" is a warning mechanism some school systems use. It is legal in most states within prescribed limitations. Parents should check the time limitation on suspension in their own state, whether it is three days, four days, or two weeks. A telephone call

to the county or area education office or the state department of public instruction office can quickly answer this
question. It is a question that the local school personnel
will evade; they don't want parents to know legal restrictions which bind the schools. Some schools will try to
bluff their way through violations of the state law in this
matter. Frequent suspension is a "scare" tactic used by
inadequate administrators to defend their inadequate
staff and program.

You should assess the situation, the school program,
the personalities of the staff, evaluate the cause of the
suspension; and if you feel that the suspension is counter-
productive and unfair, don't worry about it. Let Johnnie
have a few days' holiday from a bad scene. Don't do, as
some parents do and as the school wants you to do; don't
berate Johnnie and make him feel that he is a bad kid.
If you've decided the school's handling of the incident is
ridiculous, don't be hypocritical with Johnnie. Let him
know you remain a human being and that the whole adult
population isn't unfair, least of all his parents, the persons critically concerned with teaching Johnnie to cope
with a world that isn't always fair and just.

How do you mean? This might be a good chance for
you to teach Johnnie something about the world. He is
going to be worried and upset over the way you will
react. It is a good chance for you to explain calmly to
him that while you don't approve or condone behavior that
leads to problems of this type and that he isn't helping
himself by provoking irrational school actions, that this
is the real world. Johnnie should know that he will encounter in other schools, and in job situations, petty rules
and petty persons who enjoy muscle-flexing. You might
explore with Johnnie various methods of coping with this
kind of situation. By taking this approach, you will restore Johnnie's sense of self-dignity and his faith in adult
decency. You will be dealing with reality, and you'll be

teaching Johnnie to deal with reality. The boy needs this kind of faith in his worth at this point if he is to choose to operate as a responsible, thinking person.

What if Johnnie is a young child? Then it is even more important that you support his battered self-concept, and this might be a good chance for you to assess what Johnnie has been learning. You can find out if Johnnie is actually learning the things he should be learning at his grade level. There are all kinds of workbooks in reading and math which you could buy for this purpose. You might find that you have a few complaints about the way the school has been doing its academic job.

Aren't you being too casual or flip about this? Not at all. Suspension is used primarily in junior high and high school. Many kids at that age welcome a suspension; it is the parents the schools are aiming at. If the school does not succeed in upsetting you, if the suspension has no shock effect on you, which means no reward for the school, they won't continue to use that tactic. You should use extinction techniques on this school behavior. A behavior which is not rewarded soon extinguishes itself.

A few days off from school will not hurt any kid; don't punish him. The suspension is the punishment. Let him enjoy himself. If it's spring and he wants to go swimming or fishing, let him go. Consider those days "mental health" days. Probably he wouldn't have been suspended if he had a good school situation or if you had permitted him a few mental-health days away from a bad scene.

Expulsion—Do Not Pass Go

What are Johnnie's rights if the school does expel him? "Do Not Pass Go" is the final game in the long chain of teacher misbehaviors and other foul games leading up to it. It is game-set-match, unless you call foul, declare the game illegal, and insist on a re-match; only this time you will know the rules and what kind of players you are up against.

In some states, it is virtually illegal to expel a child from the public schools. Under the laws of some states, if a school system declares its system unsuitable for a particular child, that school system must find and finance suitable schooling for that student. A school system is not "off the hook" merely by expelling a student, but most parents don't know this. A number of states have "all-inclusive" laws which provide for the education of *all* children, no matter what label the school attaches to them.

How do I do this? Check the school code of your state or have your attorney check the school code to find out Johnnie's rights. Perhaps the school system must provide an alternative for Johnnie, even to the extent of providing him a private tutor. But you'll never hear about these rights from the local school administrators who are expelling Johnnie. The school will do everything in its power to keep from paying any fees outside its system. Many children are thrown out of school with the confident hope that the parents don't know their rights.

For a young child, you should hire a good child advocate or a nonpolitical lawyer to preserve Johnnie's rights. If you feel you cannot find a suitable lawyer or cannot afford one, check with the lawyers of the Civil Liberties Union office in your area. But it is better to spend a few dollars for a lawyer than to assume the financial burden of privately educating your child. The schools need lessons from parents on the consequences of shirking their duty. Money, they understand.

A ploy that has been used successfully by a few parents is to obtain placement for the child in a neighboring school system at their own expense. After the child is established as a tuition-paying student, the battle to force the local system to pay the tuition is begun. If you are in this situation, don't try to get him admitted to another system with the understanding that your home school system is responsible; no other system will accept him under those conditions—it's politics. And be prepared to pay the bill for a few months. This would work best if the child had been diagnosed as a special education student; if the local school booted him out, it has admitted that it is not equipped to handle his problems. Many state laws and/or the new federal public law 94-142 will force the local system to reimburse you.

What if we consider the school a lost cause for Johnnie? If you and Johnnie have decided that the school system is completely corrupt and a disaster area for Johnnie, and you don't want to fight to keep him in the system, don't despair. There are other, better alternatives for Johnnie.

If Johnnie is over sixteen-years-old, the legal age for quitting school in most states and the age after which most expulsion takes place, there is the General Education Development (GED) test that can be taken nationally. This program provides pre-testing to determine weak academic areas, and also private tutoring in those areas prior to taking the test. The tutoring is available for as long as is necessary. Upon completion of a successful test, a High School Equivalency Diploma is issued by the state in which the test is taken. Each state sets up its own guidelines concerning curriculum and scoring; but the diploma is recognized by business and industry, the military, and colleges and universities throughout the country. It is a perfectly respectable diploma with full accreditation by the state of its issuance. All this is paid for, including the tutoring, by state and federal money, as alternative education.

In larger communities, "alternative" schools are becoming more and more available to young people whom the conventional public schools have failed. These are non-conventional, individualized schools, often housed in vacant store buildings. These schools vary considerably in their purpose and role. Many of these schools are designed as an option for any student whose parents approve, not just those who don't make it in conventional schools. Many so-called "good" students who have not experienced any school problems elect this option because of the innovations. In many cases, these schools provide for student and parent input in determining curriculum, hiring and firing of staff, and expenditures of money. Some of these alternative schools utilize the open-school concept, using on-the-job training in skill areas, college and university courses, and independent study as acceptable course work toward the high-school diploma. Most alternative schools provide basic skill education and some vocational programs.

If you live in an area where alternative schools do not exist, and the child is too young for the GED, check into the new federal Office of Education "low-incidence" program which operates in all areas of the United States. This program is devoted to providing education for that small percentage of youngsters who are not provided appropriate education within their local system. This program includes all children from birth to age twenty-one. This program is interpreted differently in various states: in some states, large staffs of educators devise programs and deal directly with students, while in other states the program is liaison-oriented to help the states to provide education for all. It is your tax dollars that finance these programs and pay the salaries of the many educators employed to help your child.

Where can I get information about these options? At the local level, an anonymous phone call to the school superintendent's office or to the director of guidance could get you the information. The county or area office of education or state department of public instruction could also give you names, addresses, and telephone numbers to put you in touch with the information you seek. Or you could write to your state department of public instruction or the U.S. Office of Education in Washington for information about federal programs.

What about college? If college is your goal for Johnnie, don't be concerned because the school has expelled him. Johnnie can enter college without ever finishing high school. No matter what his IQ scores, no matter what his achievement test scores (ACT, college boards, etc.), no matter that he hasn't graduated from high school —there is a place for him. Practically every college in the country has lowered its entrance requirements. Today, anyone can attend college, public or private. No particular courses are needed, and no particular grade-point average is needed for admission. He can even become a teacher if he so chooses.

There are many colleges out there awaiting your money. Some years back, Parsons College, in Fairfield, Iowa, received a great deal of notoriety because it accepted students who could not meet admission requirements of other colleges. After several years of great financial success and great expansion, Parsons College failed, not because the approach was unsuccessful but because the North Central Association, an accrediting agency, withdrew its approval of the school. Parsons College openly admitted that it was a profit-making institution giving a "second chance" to students. This honesty offended the dainty sensitivities of the academicians everywhere else. Today, just a few years later, almost every academic institution in the nation is doing exactly what Parsons was condemned for doing in the late 1960s. The only difference is that Parsons was honest and a few years ahead of its time.

Why have the colleges lowered standards? The educational giant created to accommodate the post-World War II baby boom is now crying for students to support its giant appetite, both public and private institutions. Great pressure is placed on college and university faculties to retain students, no matter how much standards must be lowered. Admission and academic standards have been lowered to the point that anyone can go to college and almost anyone can graduate. The institution must survive, and faculty members must eat. College degrees are being granted to anyone who pays his tuition, occasionally comes to classes, and turns in a few assignments, whatever the quality. And many of these ill-prepared persons are becoming teachers in your state. You can be assured of buying Johnnie a college degree in a very free buyer's market.

If the high school should expel Johnnie, consider the possibilities of his starting college early. Some colleges do require completion of the GED for full admission, but many of these schools will permit high-school-age students to study part-time prior to graduation. The expulsion might be a blessing in disguise. Johnnie might be able to save a year or two of wasted time in a nonproductive school situation. Johnnie can get on with preparing himself for the business of living. It is not the end of the world for him. And don't think it is only the low-ability students who get expelled from school. All the research on gifted children shows that they generally have a bad time of it in the public schools. Gifted children do not respond well to Oatmeal or less-than-mediocre teachers.

Another route parents should explore in some cases is Vocational Rehabilitation if Johnnie should have a reading disability, be labeled "disturbed," or qualified in another way. Voc-Rehab will pay him to go to college or to a trade school. If Johnnie should be adjudged disabled even after the training, Voc-Rehab might even be willing to pay an employer to employ Johnnie in an on-the-job training program.

5

Hot-Air Balloons

Every child knows that the balloon that is chock-full of hot air is the one which rises the fastest and rises the highest. The best balloon is colorful and interesting; it charms and amuses. It can be playfully manipulated and behaves predictably enough so that everyone who plays with it can feel superior, but it also has just enough foibles to behave unpredictably, contrarily, and crazily enough to be interesting and laughable. Children clap their hands with glee when the balloon behaves erratically. They call it "dumb" and "silly," and it is great sport to feign fear when the balloon mindlessly strikes them on the nose; but it is all "pretend" because the balloon has no sharp edges. It is soft and "gives" whenever it comes into contact with a material object; it either gives and bounces or it explodes and is destroyed. Never is the balloon harder or tougher than its physical environment or the people who bounce it and play with it. A hot-air balloon is harmless and great sport.

What has this to do with schools? Just substitute the word "administrator" for "balloon" and the term "other educators" for the children, and the analogy is easily understood. School administrators are the best players in the survival game. Educators who have become administrators have blended into the system so smoothly that they offended nobody. They charm and amuse their superiors with their lack of sharp edges. They never try to initiate any changes; they never criticize anyone or the system itself. They applaud mediocrity and inferiority with hot-air "bravos" which support all the other hot-air balloons, causing hot-air turbulence which in turn supports themselves. That is how they manage to be promoted into school administration.

Certainly, they are not reformers or critics of the system. Administrators' creative innovation is limited to "rearranging the deck chairs on the Titanic" and calling the arrangement a "new" program, which is in actuality the same old sop rearranged. The rearrangements have names such as "open spaces," "modular scheduling," "individualized guided education," and so on. By their very nature, most administrators are incapable of making significant changes, whether from basic personality, training, or experience. They must be cooperative, pliable members of the team to be promoted and to remain on the team.

Child-advocates who see serious problems in the schools and try to do something about the problems are the fatalities of educational employment. They are systematically weeded out, or they are discredited and relegated to powerless positions if the system must keep them. Harnessed to inferiors, the child-advocates are powerless and remain as underlings as hot-air balloons soar through the heavens of the educational hierarchy.

Do you mean that all administrators are incompetent fools? No, not entirely; but in order for anyone to survive in a professional capacity as an administrator, he must be pliable enough to bend to the needs of the system, even if it means sacrificing some individual children to those needs. There are many good child-advocates in education, but they are not strong enough to survive if they attempt to stand up for a child when the needs of the system are contrary to the best interests of the child. These child-advocates need help. And the only kind of help they can get, and the best kind of help, is the help of parents. But, unfortunately, this is never communicated to the parents; and, as a consequence, many children are sacrificed to the system. Ironically, parents are considered the enemy; but they could be great friends to those who would serve children.

In private conversation, many educators will confide their disgust with the handling of a particular child. They will say, "If only the parents had objected!" Or they will say, "If that were my child, I sure would never let that happen." One principal, commenting on a cruel and inhuman kindergarten teacher who had years of experience and political expertise, said, "I kept waiting for some parents to come in and complain, but none did." This administrator had no basis for a low evaluation and firing of that cruel kindergarten teacher.

It is a matter of ethics as well as survival. The child-advocates who know the score cannot ethically bad-mouth their associates. If they do, they are labeled "troublemakers" and end up without friendly work associates and sometimes without jobs. Their hands are tied. Only the customers, you, the parents, can untie the hands of the good educators who want to help your children.

The Principal Needs a Pal

Not only are all administrators manipulated by their "superiors" in the central office, but principals are also manipulated by the teachers in their buildings. As teacher militancy and "participatory management" become stronger, the principal is more and more at the mercy of teacher-consensus. A building principal's competency and efficiency depends very heavily on the approval of him by the teachers of the building, right or wrong. He needs their approval to keep his job. He is afraid of complaints from the teachers. If too many teachers register complaints about their principal, he is removed from his job. Even if he keeps his job, the teachers can make a fool of him if they choose. There are more of them.

Timid administrators have to be forced "to take decisive action" sometimes. They must be forced by parents to "take a chance," but they need a basis for action so that they personally cannot be blamed by the system for causing trouble. Don't expect administrators to suggest or initiate "unpopular" actions which would benefit your child. But if you force them to act on your child's behalf, and you give them a defense for their ethical actions, some of them will tacitly applaud you for giving them a chance to "do the right thing." If you want an administrator "to make waves," you will first have "to rock the boat."

Professionals Need Parents

Not only are administrators hamstrung by the system but also all the other professionals, counselors, school psychologists, learning consultants, speech therapists, and so on, are likewise hamstrung. These professionals must work within the system, and they need the cooperation of all other personnel in order to get anything done for the children. Within the school organization, professionals are considered "staff" personnel as opposed to "line" personnel. The organization and terminology is much the same as that of the U.S. military. In other words, most of the ancillary, child-help personnel have no authority; they are advisory only. This organizational arrangement makes it very difficult for these persons to accomplish much for some children.

Suppose you have a school psychologist or counselor whose opinion is that a classroom teacher is behaving very badly and provoking bad behavior from a particular child who has been labeled by the school as a "problem child." Neither the school psychologist nor the counselor has any real authority and must rely on the cooperation of the "line" personnel, the principal and the teachers, to carry out any helpful program for a child. If the school psychologist or a counselor is even the slightest bit critical of a teacher's or a principal's handling of a particular child, the wrath of the criticized person can doom any suggestions the professional might make. Parent intervention at this point could greatly aid the professional in helping your child.

If a professional, whether a psychologist, counselor, or learning consultant, is critical of the school very often, his personal survival as an employee of that system is doubtful. If the professional loses his job, how can he then help any child? For these reasons, many child-help specialists suggest only what they know is "safe" within the system, whether it is right for the child or not—and thus, that would-be child-advocate becomes another hot-air balloon.

A professional's survival depends upon his serving the needs of his administrators and serving the needs of the school district. It would not be too much of a generalization to say that all school districts always need money. There is never any surplus of money in a school system. Therefore, even though the best interest of a child would be served by being put into a special program or being sent to a special program that is offered by another district, the staff professional is not likely to make this recommendation because it would cost the school district money. If a recommendation costs the school district money, this is a black mark against that professional's employment record; and he is closer to the end of his job. Therefore, many kids do not get the kind of help they should get because the child's needs do not coincide with the needs of the school system; and innocent parents never know the difference.

In addition to the financial needs of the district, the

ego needs of the administrators are a consideration. Administrators must feel that they are "right" in their personal estimation of certain kids—"Johnnie is all-bad, a troublemaker." The ancillary personnel, psychologist, consultant, whatever, may be called upon to support this kind of personal administrative judgment. If the staff professional does not uphold this commitment or philosophy that an administrator has concerning a particular child, then this professional will not be called upon again; and/or the administrator will immediately begin to work for the dismissal of the dissenting professional.

Professionals are in a strange position. In order to protect their jobs, they have to serve the administrator, they have to serve the school district's needs, and your child comes third on the list. And you must realize this whenever you are getting an opinion from one of them.

For these reasons, we feel that sometimes the only kind of valid opinion you can get is from someone not employed by the school district and not having to serve the needs of school administrators. But finding adequately qualified persons to assess your child's difficulties is only part of the problem. Professional recommendations are sometimes not followed because the school staff has already made an "investment" in its opinion of the child. They feel they must defend their opinion even if they are wrong. When the school personnel have acted according to their "vested" opinion for a period of time, it is very unpopular for a professional to contradict them.

Because the teachers and others have "vested interests" in a particular diagnosis of a child, such as "this bad child needs firm discipline," they act accordingly. When the school personnel act on this kind of negative assumption about a child, they produce in the child the kind of behavior they are looking for—at least according to their perceptions. If everyone considers a child "bad," calls him "bad," and treats him as "bad," eventually the child does become bad because that is what is expected of him; he is behaving as he is supposed to behave for them.

·   *How can I help the child-advocate?* Sometimes it is necessary for parents to "read between the lines" when consulting with a school professional. Victimized professionals cannot always say the things they would like to say for fear of offending the school. But they will drop hints sometimes that you should be open to. If a child-advocate has been trying to help your child, but others within the system are torpedoing those efforts, you've got to step in.

The learning specialist has told you in private conference: "I feel that it would be helpful to Johnnie if he began cursive writing now instead of manuscript printing, but that is not the way his teacher handles it." The specialist is telling you something—she is telling you that the teacher simply will not cooperate with her. For your child's sake, you must step in and help the child-advocate by applying Parental Persistence.

"It's not our philosophy."

Seven-year-old Johnnie, who has above-average intelligence, has experienced extreme difficulties in printing manuscript letters, primarily letter reversals. The learning specialist from the county education office has evaluated Johnnie's problem and diagnosed the problem as an organic perceptual problem. Ms. Learned Specialist recommended to the classroom teachers and to you that Johnnie proceed to learn cursive handwriting, as opposed to manuscript printing. In cursive handwriting, the letter reversals will not occur because practiced cursive letter formations do not permit it. Besides, Johnnie will not need to produce perfect manuscript printing as an adult anyway. This makes good sense to you, and you are grateful to the learning consultant for proposing such a simple solution to the problem.

But, a week after the specialist has proposed the

change to the classroom teachers, you discover that Johnnie is still struggling with failing attempts to correct the letter reversals in manuscript printing. Johnnie has exploded at school and refused to do the work; and he tells you he hates school, hates writing, and that he does not ever want to learn to write. The school has labeled him stubborn and uncooperative. You must step in. Go see Ms. Fila Sophy.

> YOU: Ms. Fila Sophy, I understand that Johnnie is still working on manuscript printing and that he is still having difficulty with it. He has brought home several sheets of paper filled with his efforts to print "b" and "d" correctly, and he still does not perceive the difference and he is still reversing them. Ms. Learned Specialist recommended that he learn to write in cursive to solve the problem of letter reversals. I want you to follow her recommendations.

> MS. FILA SOPHY: Yes, he has been very stubborn and uncooperative. And I am going to start him on cursive writing, but first he must learn to distinguish and reproduce all of the letters properly. And that's what we're working on now. [She obviously missed the point of Ms. Specialist's recommendation—either through stupidity or uncooperative stubbornness.]

> YOU: But Ms. Specialist recommended that he learn cursive writing *instead* of continuing with manuscript printing. You are continuing to force him into continued failure to do what is perceptually impossible for him. I want you to begin immediately to follow Ms. Specialist's recommendation. [Let's see who is stubborn and uncooperative.]

> MS. FILA SOPHY: But Mrs. Parent, we feel that

a child must thoroughly learn manuscript printing before he is allowed to proceed to cursive writing. It is not good to leave one task uncompleted to start another one. He is not ready to learn cursive writing yet.

YOU: I understand you feel that way, but you evidently missed the point of Ms. Specialist's recommendation. She is a specialist in learning problems of this type, and she has accomplished success for many children through her recommendations. I insist that you follow her recommendations.

MS. FILA SOPHY: [Loudly and exasperated.] But, Mrs. Parent, that is not our philosophy here. [That is supposed to stop you dead in your tracks. How do you argue with someone's philosophy? Don't lose your cool, and don't argue philosophy with her.]

YOU: I understand that is your philosophy, but I want you to immediately implement Ms. Specialist's suggestion with my son. [You don't try to argue the merits of her philosophy with her. That is a dead-end conversation.]

MS. FILA SOPHY: There are many different theories and approaches to teaching, and I happen not to share Ms. Specialist's opinion.

YOU: I understand there are many different theories, but I want you to follow the recommendation of Ms. Specialist for Johnnie.

MS. FILA SOPHY: Well, it won't work, and I don't want to be party to it. [She still wants you to argue the merits of various approaches to impress you with her superior knowledge. Don't.]

YOU: I understand how you feel, but I want Johnnie to start learning cursive writing. [You repeat yourself as long as it takes to convince her that you won't get sidetracked into a discussion of theories and methods.]

MS. FILA SOPHY: I suppose I can try, but I promise you it won't work. [This is designed to threaten you for making educational decisions for your child.]

YOU: Good, and will you start with it immediately and do the very best job you can in teaching cursive writing to Johnnie so that the recommendation has every chance to work?

MS. FILA SOPHY: [Daunted and indignant.] Of course; I always do the best job I can for any student.

YOU: Oh, fine; I'll be looking for Johnnie's papers to come home, and I'll be checking with you in a week or so to talk with you about it again. [You've let her know that this is not the end of it and that you will be monitoring her efforts.]

If the teacher had not backed down finally and had not agreed to follow the professional's recommendation, you could have backed her into the position of labeling herself as noncooperative, defiant, or belligerent.

TEACH-THE-TEACHER TACTIC

YOU: Then I understand you absolutely refuse to cooperate with the highly trained learning specialists from the county office. If that is the case, I want you to put that in writing for me so that I can get proper education for Johnnie.

No teacher wants to openly defy another professional, especially one better trained and in a higher-level job than he or she. Since you knew before you went to school that the teacher was directly violating the professional's recommendations, you should take a tape recorder with you so that the violation, defiance, and lack of cooperation will be on record. The very presence of the tape recorder would in most cases keep the teacher from openly refusing.

What could I do with the tape even if I did record it all? Take this tape to the principal, the superintendent of schools, or to a school board member and demand that the professional's recommendations be followed. The administrators would accede to your request because they don't want to have their relationship with other educational agencies jeopardized.

Ms. Fila Sophy will have to be closely monitored for the next few weeks as she does apparently cooperate. A teacher who is forced to do something she doesn't want to do can display a great deal of "passive resistance." Make sure she does not get away with that either. If all else fails, you can always teach your child cursive writing yourself with the aid of the many workbooks printed for this purpose.

How can I distinguish between the child-advocates and the hot-air balloons? Find out what you can about the conditions under which the professional works, the attributes, philosophies, and so on, of his or her superiors, and the needs of the district. This can be done in a number of ways, but a good place to start is to ask direct questions of the professional, such as: "What is your case load? Can you easily handle that many? Could you take on more children? How is your work load determined? Does the administration (superintendent, principal, curriculum director, etc.) have any specialized training in, understanding of, experience in, or sympathy for your particular specialty? How much money from the local operating budget is allocated to your particular area, beyond state and federal requirements and special subsidized programs?" If administrators have any training, experience, or even a knowledgeable understanding of a specialized area, they will lend support to it, will support the professionals who work in the area, and will work to allocate adequate funds to support a program.

If you get glib, affirmative answers to all of these questions indicating that everything is par excellence, don't believe it. The professional is either stupid or a hot-air balloon. If the answers you get are tentative, attempting to be honest, but stopping short of direct criticism, you are probably dealing with a sensitive, intelligent professional who would be a child-advocate if he or she possibly could.

Another way to obtain this information is from professionals in the same specialty who work at the county or regional office, or even at the state department level if you have access to those people. County professionals and sometimes private practitioners will sometimes tell you a great deal about individual administrators, system philosophies, and even, occasionally, other professionals. They have a wealth of information because they have been trying to perform their jobs through the same persons. Their jobs are more secure than those of the local school professionals whose jobs may be at stake if they criticize their bosses or the system that employs them.

Other parents of children with similar problems can be founts of information, especially parents whose children are older and who have been battling the system for years to get help. Check around the community to find out names of several of these people, and then telephone them.

If the speech and hearing specialist has a case load large enough for five speech specialists, this lack of adequate staff is going to affect the professional's ability to help your child. Maybe your child, who is in need of special help, will be turned away or treated only super-

ficially—perhaps by volunteers—because for economy
reasons the speech and hearing section is understaffed.

Can they do this—turn kids away? They do it all the
time. In many states it is illegal, but they do it anyway.
The chief method for circumventing laws requiring specialized help for all children who need it is simply not to
acknowledge that a particular child needs help. This keeps
the case load down to fit into what the school system has
decided it can "afford" for that particular specialty.

In one instance, volunteer high school students per-
formed all of the actual speech therapy for a school district. This was in a state that mandates speech and hearing help. The local school system employed only one speech
therapist who diagnosed all the children in the district,
a district large enough to need six full-time therapists,
but speech and hearing was not ranked very high on the
priority list. The sole therapist "trained" the high-school
volunteers who were the only persons to work directly
with the children. This ruse for circumventing the law did
not work for long because the high school kids were intelligent enough to know that they didn't know enough to
be doing the work, and most of the volunteers quit. This
kind of misuse of volunteers is not unusual. Parents don't
have to put up with this kind of shenanigan. Parents can
force the school to obey the laws which protect children
by requiring appropriate instruction. This topic, however,
is treated in the chapter on special education.

Parents should also appraise any child specialist's
training for the job he has. Find out what his training is,
where he received it, when he received it, and what degrees he holds. It is especially important to find out what
field the actual degrees are in. There are many persons
today who hold degrees in one field but are working in
another field, related, perhaps, but not with the proper
preparation. Find out the professional's orientation in his

field; there are many opposing theories in most professional specialty areas. One method of treatment might work for your child, and another method might not work. The best professionals are eclectic in orientation; this means they have not locked themselves into one method. They do not suffer from tunnel vision; they use a variety of methods. If a professional is eclectic, he will generally say so. Naturally, he will consider some methods better than others; but his mind is not closed.

Those who were trained many years ago and who have not kept abreast of the vast new research and methods are obsolete. This does not say that all old methods are obsolete because some of the old methods are superior to some of the new, untested methods. But a good professional has an open mind and will pick and choose from available theories and methods, both new and old. In fact, this is one of the problems for many of the new, young professionals. Many of them have been taught only the newest, most popular fad-approach to their field. Some of the older, experienced professionals have seen the fads come and go; but they have also distilled and assimilated the valuable research and worthwhile methods over the years. They, therefore, have much more to offer a kid with a problem than some of the hot-air balloon set.

In appraising a child specialist, one of the best ways to find out whether or not he is any good is to check out his "track record." Has he really helped any kids? Ask around your neighborhood, your community, to find out what you can about his reputation. Probably the best way to find out the reputation of a school professional is to contact members of some of the special-interest parent groups. And this does not mean the PTA. Members of local chapters of organizations such as the Council on Exceptional Children (CEC) and the Association for Children with Learning Disabilities (ACLD) are a fountain of information about local professionals.

What can I do if I get a "bad" appraisal report on a professional? Don't let that person work with your child. The "wrong" professional can do more damage than good. A child with problems does not need another bumbling incompetent. If you have nosed around enough to get a derogatory report, you've already explored channels for finding appropriate help. Good professional help is generally available, but the trick is finding it. In some cases, parents might decide to obtain an opinion, and in addition, treatment from a professional child advocate in private practice. In fact, because of all of the politics involved in school systems, some educators believe that the only honest diagnostic opinion is one obtained from a professional in private practice.

A String of Balloons

Parents should familiarize themselves with the hierarchy of the school, which is simply the line of command, or chain of command. Figure 5-1 in this chapter explains the organization graphically, but this is not the total story. There is always an uncharted network of politics operating within every school system. The more that parents can learn about these unofficial policies, opinions, views, friendships, and enmities, the more he can do to help his child. School administrators even have an official name for this network; they call it the informal organizational chart.

I know what "politics" means, but what has this to do with my child? Suppose your neighborhood school has a teacher whose brutal treatment of children is well-known within the community but nothing is done about her. She might be best of friends with the building principal. Their friendly compatibility might seem incongruous because the principal appears to be a true child-advocate. You would need one more piece of information to understand it. The brutal teacher happens to be the sister of the president of the local school board, or she might be the wife of the county superintendent of schools. You know how it goes.

Even if he wanted to do so, the principal could not get rid of that bad teacher. But you can. Your job does not depend on it. You might find a lot of support within the system if you were to initiate action. Your use of Parental Persistence to have your child removed from Ms. Brutal's classroom would do your child a great favor and, at the same time, give the principal some ammunition to use to get rid of a bad teacher. Enough Parental Persistence from many parents could do it.

If the school curriculum director has a rigid, lock-step philosophy, which he insists that all teachers follow, whether it is good for all children or not, every teacher in that district is going to have to comply with his dictates no matter how many children suffer from it. If you were to use Parental Persistence to demand alternative instruction, a diet other than Oatmeal for your child, you would find the teachers resistant, perhaps, at first; but if they were convinced you meant business, you might find that you have support from them. They can "blame" you as they deviate from the dictator's curriculum to help your child.

Why is the U.S. Office of Education hanging out by itself in the chart with no strings tying it to the states? Although we have a United States Office of Education, which is part of the Department of Health, Education, and Welfare, we do not have a federal school system in the United States. Our federal constitution does not provide for a national school system; therefore, this is a function left to the individual states. As a consequence, we have fifty separate school systems in the United States.

Since the founding of this nation, the Office of Education has been a bastard-child, shunted from department to department and changing its name frequently. In 1953, it finally found a home as part of the Department of Health, Education, and Welfare. And each year this office grows stronger; today, even though we still do not have a national school system, the Office of Education has personnel scattered in hundreds of offices throughout the nation. Although its role is still advisory and contributory, by way of special programs that role is changing. The monetary contributions of the federal government have strings attached, and there is an increasing atmosphere of obligation developing, largely due to financial pressure. Some educators fear that, in time, Congress will pass legislation which will wipe out the autonomy of the state educational systems. A federal school system would encumber our schools with even more bureaucracy than they have now.

The State Legislatures

The ultimate authority for education lies in each of the fifty state legislatures. The legislature determines very general guidelines for the schools in such areas as curriculum; finance; election or appointment of state boards of education; state superintendent; local boards; teacher certification, and so on. The legislature passes the laws which control all the other educational agencies, only some of which you hear about.

State Board of Education

The state board of education, generally appointed by the governor, determines school policy within the limits of laws passed by the legislature. This board in many states appoints the state superintendent of public instruction or commissioner of education, however he is called. There are still some states which elect the chief officer at general election.

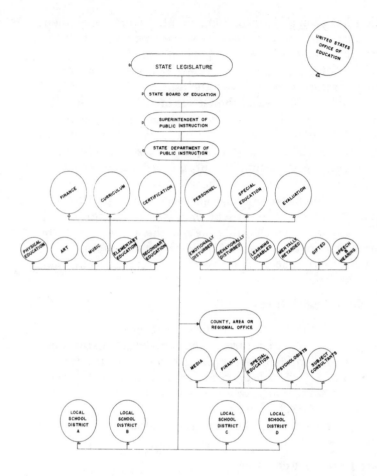

Figure 5-1   Hot-air balloons

State Superintendent of Public Instruction

The superintendent of public instruction is, in essence, the chief state executive of the schools and has a vast army of persons working for him in the state department of public instruction. Working within the general laws and policies created by the legislature and the state board of education, the many departments of the department of public instruction interpret and implement laws and policies and make sure that the schools of the state meet minimum standards. For all practical purposes, the power for running the schools lies at this level. But this power is given by the people through their elected representatives.

State Department of Public Instruction

Parents should not hesitate to approach appropriate persons at the department of public instruction (DPI) level if they are convinced that their child has been cheated of his rights by the local school system. Working at this level can be effective for two reasons: local school systems are extremely fearful of censure from DPI; and the DPI itself is a political animal extremely fearful of public criticism, especially if parents were to threaten lawsuit against it or any of its local systems, with the resulting adverse publicity.

There are often some very good, dedicated persons working at various levels of the DPI who are child-advocates. Most of the people working at the state level are former teachers, administrators, and child specialists. They have risen through the political ranks to the positions they hold. No matter what facet of the schools about which you might be concerned, there are appropriate persons at the state level you could consult.

County, Regional, or Area Offices

This intermediate office has evolved from the historic county offices of education, many of which are now being merged together to form regional or area offices. In most places today, these agencies do not have any real authority, but rather they exist as service agencies to the independent school districts within their boundaries.

These offices provide services which are impractical for each of the small school districts to provide for itself.

Psychologists, learning consultants, guidance consultants, speech and hearing therapists, and so on, are among the persons employed by many service offices to provide advice to member school districts when requested. Some area offices maintain media libraries, consisting of films, tapes, recordings, and books which are lent to the requesting school systems. Data-processing facilities are also sometimes provided to the member districts for processing their report cards, financial records, and others.

Parents should be aware of these services because sometimes help for a child is available at this level when it is not available from the local school system. Because there is frequently an overlap of services from the local district and the area service office, professional jealousies and territorial conflicts sometimes keep a child from receiving the best help available. If parents are not satisfied with the handling of their child at the local district level, those parents should enlist the help of appropriate persons from the county, area, or regional office.

Local School Board and Superintendent

The local school board is the creation of the state legislature. Although local school boards are required to enforce state laws governing schools, the local board has considerable leeway for determining the quality of education in the local community. State laws draw only minimal guidelines.

The elected members of local school boards function as policy-makers for the school district. Since in many states the local superintendent of schools functions as the executive officer of the school board, although without a vote, the school board leans very heavily on his advice. The school-board members are your representatives for controlling the local schools. Unless school-board members receive input from parents, they will generally rubber-stamp any proposal—other than financial—that the school administrators suggest.

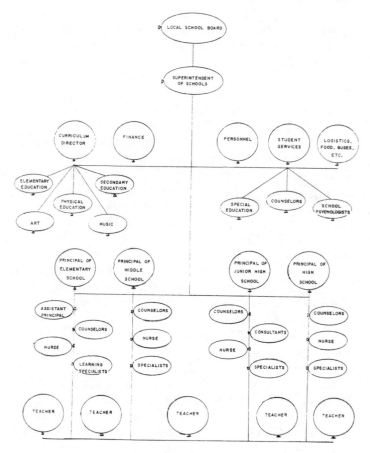

Figure 5-2   Local system of balloons simplified

School board members are laymen, noneducators, just like you; and they are not well informed about all the problems within the schools, especially problems of individual students. Sometimes parents can obtain justice for their child by merely requesting it from the local school board. This can be done via private, informal conference with one or more members of the board or by formal request to the full board at a regular board meeting. It is an avenue for obtaining justice that parents should not neglect.

If you should consider petitioning your representative on the school board, do not reveal this to the school personnel with whom you are in conflict. If you do, the threatened party will rush to fill board members' ears with a highly biased report of the situation. By the time you do talk with the board member, he might be so prejudiced toward your child that he cannot hear what you are saying, especially if your Johnnie has been painted "ugly," and you a "radical dingbat." Educators call their part in this process "covering yourself," a term too frequently heard in educational circles. If you decide to use this approach to help your child, assess the individual board members. Through your research concerning personalities and politics among the board members, decide which person would be most receptive to your problem.

Some school board members are persons who are also hot-air balloons. This type is generally among the majority faction of the board which automatically rubber-stamps what the school administration dictates, and may be so ignorant that he doesn't have any ideas of his own. But let's give him the benefit of the doubt and say that he is generally well-intentioned, community minded—but a personality who always "plays it safe" and doesn't believe in unpopular issues. Such a board member convinces himself that the school system is "all good" and that there is very little need for change; he moves only when a large segment of the community demands a change. It is at this point that he generally loses his position on the board to another person backed by the dissenting community. It is possible that you might find a receptive spirit among the majority faction, but it is not likely. For them, anyone who criticizes the status quo must be a "nut" because these people *are* the status quo. They represent the school system as it is. They are merely doing their duty in perpetuating the system as it is and, perhaps, raking off some indirect financial gain by influencing contracts and so on.

Another type of board member who may or may not be a member of the majority faction is the glory-seeker, the novice politician on his way up to more important political office—the grandstander. This type is interested primarily in his own image, his own importance. He may do some "boat-rocking," but he chooses which boats he rocks according to whether or not the action gives him personally what he seeks: glory, attention, and news coverage. He might be of some help to your child, but only if there is something in it for him personally. But you cannot depend on him because he is very busy with his posturing for the press.

On almost every school board, there is a minority faction or at least one person who is a true child-advocate and wants the best for each child, regardless of politics. This kind of person does not concern himself with how his attitude will be accepted by others on the board or by the school administrators, but does make it his business to become informed about what is actually going on in the schools, and will not be a rubber stamp because of his ignorance. He thinks for himself and will generally give an objective hearing to any member of the community. This person would be a good person to be informed of your problem and to thoroughly understand it. If he understands the problem, and agrees with you, he will do whatever he can to help.

Local System Superintendent

School superintendents are balloons that come in just about every shape and color. Some are highly authoritarian, and others are democratic in their leadership; but the trend today is toward the democratic type, especially since the rise of teacher-militancy and the advent of participatory management. There are good and bad of both types;

but with teacher-militancy and its demands, the superintendent, who represents the board as management, is doing less managing every year. Today, school boards and the top school administration are finding it increasingly expedient to bow to the militant dictates of teachers.

The average time a school superintendent spends in any one school system is about eight years, whether he is the builder-of-new-buildings type or the educator-interested-in-children type. Because of this occupational ax over his head, the superintendent's chief motivation is to lengthen his tenure as much as possible. The mark of a good school administrator is to keep a low profile, which means not to become involved in any real controversy and not to generate any adverse newspaper publicity.

Today, the "team" approach to school administration is popular. More and more frequently, the top administrator insists that his immediate subordinates support the team decisions. The team approach naturally makes for more comfortable working conditions and expedites implementation of policy but, at the same time, it gags dissent and prohibits new or better ideas. Team innovation is too often limited to safe "rearrangements of the furniture."

In the last few years, except through the firing of athletic coaches and making unpopular demands for bond referendums, the major source of trouble for superintendents has come from the teachers within the system. A superintendent who is not supported by the teachers soon finds himself without a job. The teachers manage to embroil him in controversy with them and cast him as the "heavy." Simultaneously, they bad-mouth him throughout the community, causing his eventual resignation or dismissal. More than one superintendent has been fired by a community when he was trying to improve the schools for the children of those who were manipulated into demanding his resignation.

Educational failure, from the child's standpoint, can

be attributed largely to weak, ineffective management who fear organized, militant teachers and criticism from the community, competitive ideas within the administration, experimentation, and, even worse, fear to admit that an experiment was a mistake. Unfortunately, when a school administrator does commit himself to a trivial new idea, he often irrationally defends it until his resignation or dismissal.

The Superintendent's Team

The number of persons on the superintendent's staff depends on the size of the school system. In small school systems, the superintendent performs all of the functions with the help of a secretary or two. In larger systems, many persons are delegated specific responsibilities. Although the organization of the various school systems varies considerably, the chart in Figure 5-2 is typical. The directors of each of the subcategories are technically staff personnel; and what power they have they derive from the superintendent, according to his philosophies and policies. The chief role for each of these persons is to coordinate the activities for the particular speciality in the various buildings of the district.

Parents traditionally have very little contact with the superintendent's team, but they do occasionally hear the names from teachers and others. Functionally speaking, the directors of curriculum, student services, and special education, are the "bosses" of the professionals working with the children. Naturally, the philosophies and viewpoints, attitudes and needs of the bosses affect the work of the child specialists. Because these staff persons technically have little autonomous authority, their decisions and judgements reflect the needs of the team more than the needs of individual children. However, if parents feel they are getting the "run around" at the school building level, they may get better answers and possibly more results by talking with the appropriate person at this specialist level. Sometimes parents can find at the specialist level solutions with which personnel at the building level are not aware. Your demands that the specialists provide for your child's needs can "free" the specialist to perform, despite team goals to the contrary.

In order to understand your own particular school system, it would be wise to request a copy of the system's organizational chart with names. If copies are not available, you have the right to look at the official chart and take notes on anything that concerns your child at the moment. All school systems have an organizational chart which is generally located, if no place else, at the central administrative offices.

6

Teacher Disabilities & Limitations (Special Education)

Special Education is a highly complex, misunderstood, and often mishandled area of education. Stereotyped impressions of what special education is and is not exist in the minds of both parents and educators, and most of these are wrong. Special education is baffling even to the specially trained workers in the field as well as to parents and other regular educators.

To dispel the most erroneous and predominant myth, special education is *not* a program for only the mentally incompetent, for the hopelessly feebleminded souls. Special education *is* an all-inclusive term for any kind of extra resource that any extraordinary child might need, ranging from programs for the highly gifted child to those for the severely retarded child or young adult. That spectrum includes the whole range of human intelligence. No parent should be ashamed or reluctant to seek special help for his child.

It is true that specific labels such as "emotionally disturbed," "maladjusted," "learning disabled," and so on, for children do exist and, unfortunately, are attached to the child who receives special help. But the trend is away from this labeling approach, which is one of the good, healthy changes within the schools today. The only reason that these labels still exist and that special education leaders tolerate them is that the labels are needed to convince congressmen and school boards to pass laws and to allocate the money needed to provide special services to children who need them. Protectors of educational purse strings can be convinced to allocate money to "disabled" children, whereas they are not receptive to providing "extra" money for children who have historically been considered the "bad kids" or the "troublemakers." Therefore, special-education workers accept some label indicating a handicap for the child in exchange for the money they can get to help the child.

If all the children who need the special services of special educators were identified and funds were available to provide these services, special education would be provided to about a third of the school population—maybe more. Astounding figure, is it? Not really. It is more of a derogatory comment on our educational system than a comment on the prevalence of abnormalities in children.

Our basic educational system and most of our methods of educating were designed over a hundred years ago, and have not changed much since that time. Until recently, any child who did not respond positively to the Oatmeal educational program was simply thrown out of the schools. No one questioned this. Thomas Edison was labeled a "dunce" and thrown out of the American schools after only three months. It was not Edison's fault that the school could not teach him; it was a fault of the school. Today we throw them out or label them as "bad" kids.

Special education has developed over the years as an effort of the schools to make patchwork repairs to the basic educational program, to make amends for the limitations of Oatmeal. This is a great deal like the proliferation of fruit-flavored, presweetened, oatmeal-base cereals available at the grocery store. The patching of the basic program has been necessary because we persist in viewing our educational system as a sacred cow, something that cannot be touched or corrected, let alone rebuilt. Rather than admit that the Oatmeal-based educational program has faults and limitations, we label as abnormal any child who does not respond to it.

Actually, all education should be special education. No two of us are alike. Our learning abilities, styles, motivations, and goals all differ as much as we differ in facial appearance. We all know that some things are difficult for us to learn, but we can learn them. We all know that we learn in different ways—that under certain kinds of instruction we can learn, and under other kinds of instruction we cannot learn. Some subject matter that we were simply not interested in learning when we were young is now of considerable interest to us. Why? Maybe we needed a special kind of education. Maybe we needed a special teacher. Perhaps all teachers should be special-education teachers.

Our schools have traditionally tried to teach only that mythical "average" child, seemingly assuming that children are assembly-line produced. Any child who is "different" is considered defective and rejected (i.e., relegated to the "don't expect anything of them" heap). Why do our schools encourage all children to "be like all the other children"? To make teachers' work easier! Are the great inventions created by the average person? Are the great ideas and solutions to world problems discovered by the average person? Are the great industries built by the average person? Of course not! Our educational system's worship of the average and lack of regard for the "special" aspects of children is in reality public-enemy-number-one!

It is easy to identify the blind, the deaf, the severely retarded, the crippled, and the multiply-handicapped because their differences are physical and highly visible. Society has long recognized that these children have special needs; and the schools have for many years made attempts, although not always adequate, to provide for them. These are the persons that the public associates with the term "special education." This group is statistically quite small compared to the general population. Both the parents and the schools know who these kids are very early and work to provide for their education. Parents of these children very early have had to become quite knowledgeable concerning their child's education. Therefore, this group will not be discussed here.

In recent years, research has proven that there are a lot of other children who are also "different" and need an education that is different from the Oatmeal diet concocted for that mythical average child. In fact, every year educational and psychological research is discovering and identifying more variances within the realm of human learning that call for special education. The problem with the vast majority of these kids is that they are more normal than they are abnormal. They appear, by traditional standards, to be like every other child. But they do have learning differences that have confounded the schools because these kids just don't "make it" in the schools. They are the children who fail, the children who drop out, the children who cause trouble. In short, they are the "problem" kids.

None of them would have to be problem kids if their educations were tailored to fit their individual needs. But before appropriate special education can be tailored, these kids must first be identified and their specific problems diagnosed. Because of educators' ignorance concerning these nonvisible special needs, educators' addiction to and defense of Oatmeal, or educators' bowing to financial pressures, most of these kids are not receiving the kind of special assistance they need. It is to the parents of these children, who do battle with the schools every day and sometimes live in a virtual hell, that this chapter is directed. If parents can recognize more of the children's needs, parents can then seek appropriate education for their children.

What nonvisible kids are you talking about? The gifted, the talented, the learning-disabled, the emotionally disturbed, the behaviorally disordered, and the socially maladjusted. This group has one common denominator the public generally does not associate with special education —unlimited potential, both intellectual and creative, which will be wasted because of the schools' inability to accept them as productive human beings and to cope with their differences. The schools label these kids as "weirdos," or "problem kids," and relegate them to the nonproductive human trash heap, little realizing that one of them might be another Thomas Edison, another Meredith Wilson, another Sylvia Plath, another Vachel Lindsey, or Louis Pasteur who is being discarded. By such action, the school is providing clients for our overcrowded prisons and mental hospitals.

Gifted

Who are the gifted? Every state school system or agency which acknowledges the gifted has a different definition for this group, but they all agree that a gifted child is one who is intellectually superior. For all practical purposes, this group is the top 2 percent of the population intellectually as scored on intelligence tests. Some authorities, such as Samuel Kirk, describe the gifted as those scoring above 140 on intelligence tests. Others set the score at 135, but the number depends on which test is used because there is variance in tests as explained in the chapter on School Records and Test Scores. On the Wechsler Intelligence Scale for Children (WISC), only 2 percent of the population scores above 130. The numbers really do not matter a great deal here, except for legal purposes in defining these children. Most authorities agree that the small group obtaining scores anywhere near any of these numbers is gifted.

Probably the most neglected group who deserve special education is the gifted. Who feels sorry for them? Many of them enter kindergarten knowing how to read, while other children struggle to learn this task over a period of several years. No academic task is difficult for them to learn in a very short period of time. They are intellectually several years ahead of the other children in their age group. The gifted child of four or five years has the reasoning capacity and often the skills of the average child twice his age. But most school systems make no provision for this child when he starts school.

Because of state school laws setting a chronological age when a child starts school, no matter what the child's developmental variation or intellectual variation, starting school is sometimes a big shock to the gifted. For many of them, adjustment to school means putting up with doing boring, repetitive tasks that were long ago mastered, learning not to embarrass the teacher or the other children by revealing mastery of the task at hand or the next few tasks. Adjustment means also learning not to get caught talking to neighbors, learning how to alleviate the boredom without being punished, and maybe learning to conceal contempt for the school and even the comparative slowness of the other children.

First-grader Jean Louise's difficulties with her teacher in *To Kill a Mockingbird* reveal the gifted child's dilemma: "As I read the alphabet a faint line appeared between [the teacher's] eyebrows, and after making me read most of *My First Reading* and the stock market quotations from *The Mobile Register* aloud, she discovered that I was literate and looked at me with more than faint distaste. Miss Caroline told me to tell my father not to teach me any more, it would interfere with my reading ... 'You tell him I'll take over from here and try to undo the damage.' ... I knew I had annoyed Miss Caroline, so

I let well enough alone and stared out the window until recess ... I was bored, so I began a letter to Dill. Miss Caroline caught me writing and told me to tell my father to stop teaching me. 'Besides,' she said, 'We don't write in first grade, we print.' You won't learn to write until you're in third grade!' "

These children often become so turned off by school that they lose all interest in formal learning and express decided aversion to continuing in school any longer than they must. This means that they sometimes reject college entirely. This particular situation is not only a personal tragedy but also a national tragedy in that we lose the contributions these gifted might make. We are also stuck with being served by a more mediocre mentality in our highly trained professionals, for only the mediocre can survive so much regimented schooling.

What should be done about this gifted group? Every school system should provide a special program for these students; and the major component of the program should be a gifted teacher, a person possessing high intelligence, high creativity, emotional security, and enthusiasm for learning. Only a gifted teacher is equipped to teach these children; a program for the gifted is doomed to failure if it is administered and taught by persons who are intellectually inferior to their students. The teacher of only average mentality cannot possibly grasp the learning styles, the reasoning, or the depth of a gifted child, let alone his or her sensitivity, sense of humor, and originality. Gifted children suffer through their school days primarily because so very few teachers are gifted.

Unfortunately, most so-called programs for the gifted have turned out rather badly, primarily because of the design of the program. Too many of the programs have confused quantity with quality and have simply loaded these brilliant children with the task of doing the same material as all the other kids, only six times as much.

The only learning theory to defend this is faculty psychology, a theory refuted in the 1890s by William James. This punitive tactic is tantamount to harnessing thoroughbred race horses to haul wagons of concrete. It is the mediocre mind's understanding of genius.

Some school systems that flatter themselves into thinking their program is "individualized" create equally disastrous programs for the gifted. A school system that uses programmed instructional materials, such as the Sullivan Reading Series, magnanimously allows gifted children to complete these materials as rapidly as they can. Horrible! All programmed materials are designed for the least intelligent person who might be using them—they are pitched to the lowest common denominator. Programmed materials assume no intellectual insight, no intuitive leaps—no brains. They are designed about the way the U.S. income tax forms are designed—and are about as interesting. All the research proves that programmed texts are wrong for even the moderately intelligent child, let alone the gifted. Teaching based only on programmed instruction is no teaching at all.

Naturally, a program for the gifted must devote appropriate attention to basic skills; but the children should be allowed more individual choice than the usual student in the pursuit of special projects. The program should allow for both horizontal enrichment and vertical acceleration. By traditional standards, gifted children might cover course work for three grades in one year. Unfortunately, mediocre schools and mediocre teachers devote most of their energies to "slowing down" these kids. The least they could do would be to allow the kids to use the time their native brilliance has saved on scholarly pursuits they choose themselves according to their own interests.

A social studies unit for the gifted should not include more facts and dates to be memorized. Rather, the children should be encouraged to use their minds, to explore the "whys" and "hows" of history, and be allowed to conjecture about alternative outcomes of events in history, such as "How did Napoleon's ambition affect American independence?" and "What might have been the fate of the American continent if France had seriously contested the British for control of it?" This sort of brainstorming should be done in lively small-group discussions. Research of facts should be preparation for these discussions, and not deadly copious copying of encyclopedia articles—alas, another typical teacher's error in occupying the time of gifted children.

Although there is merit in keeping gifted children in the regular schools and mingled to a certain extent with regular children, they should be permitted ample opportunity for classes with each other to provide the kind of interplay and stimulation their superior and active minds need. These special classes, within the regular school structure, should be kept small. In order to keep children in the neighborhood schools, multi-age grouping might be necessary. An average neighborhood school might conceivably have a class of eight or ten students or two classes of four or five each with an age mix. Within this system of special classes, and especially in schools that provide no special classes of this sort, children should be allowed to skip grades.

Will the schools permit this? Some will, and some will not. It depends on the laws of the state, and it depends on the philosophy of the school system. Oddly enough, the same teacher, the same principal, the same school philosophy that will suggest to you that Johnnie should stay in second grade another year because of developmental lag or difference, will often object strenuously if you suggest that Suzie ought to skip second grade. Educators seem to understand that some children learn more slowly than the average and would benefit from slowing down the pace of their education. But those same educators are blind to the needs of the other extreme, those children who would benefit from speeding up the pace of their education.

The school's major objection to the academic acceleration of gifted children is on the basis of emotional and social development. Although acknowledging intellectual advancement, some schools will lecture parents on the importance of Suzie's remaining with her age-mates so that she will not suffer emotionally and socially. This is the favorite guilt-hook schools use for manipulating parents of gifted children to defend the school's wasting of the child's time; they will try to make you feel that you are trying to rob Suzie of her childhood. This is a bunch of bunk and parents should know it. All of the research, including Terman's studies of gifted children, has proven that the social adjustment made by gifted students with one to three years of grade advancement was superior to that of their classmates. Intellectually advanced children are generally emotionally and socially advanced also. The majority of them are also physically advanced for their chronological age. It has been found that these children get along better with children one to three years older than they.

If these children skip several years of school, what happens to them as high school graduates at age fourteen or fifteen? These are the children who certainly should and, in all likelihood, will study for advanced degrees and at professional schools, spending anywhere from seven to ten years studying beyond the high school level. After an early high-school graduation, these children can begin their college training early, saving anywhere from one to three years of wasted time. Today, most parts of the country are served by commuter junior colleges or private colleges within a short distance of any child's home. These "children" can continue to live at home with the security of their parents while they complete the first two to four years of undergraduate work. By that time, they will be eighteen or twenty years old, and even the most narrow-minded persons in our lockstep society will not frown on their leaving home to pursue professional training. There is nothing sacred about our present twelve-year organizational plan for education, elementary through high school. It was originated by Comenius during the Renaissance and has remained a tradition. It is not based on any research of the human mind, or even on any well-conceived theories.

Won't these kids feel "different"? Yes, they *are* "different." No matter what the schools do with them, they will feel different anyway. Even if they are held back to the same lockstep curriculum of their age-mates, they will feel "different" and be viewed as "different" by their peers. And not only will they be wasting precious time and potential, but they very likely will find other ways to occupy their minds and their time—and maybe not good ways. Many of the kids caught up in the recent drug cult were brilliant, talented kids who were bored and contemptuous of the way they were treated.

How do I go about obtaining proper placement for my gifted child? The first step is to check your state's school laws to determine whether or not there is provision for the gifted. Also check the laws for "all-inclusive" provisions such as "appropriate education for *all* children." If such a provision exists in your state, then you should use Parental Persistence to obtain appropriate grade placement and educational program.

Naturally, it is important that a gifted child be officially identified. It is best to have this done either privately or through a state or county (or area or regional) agency which is not beholden to your local school system. Local school systems often identify "special children" according to the system's needs, not the child's needs. If a gifted program does not exist within the system, that system simply will not have identified any children who need a special program. Or if the system has only limited space in its program for the gifted, children in excess of that space will not be identified.

If no provision is made for these children by the state or by your local school system and you have no legal backing, you should look to private education for your child. Private schools which make provision for brilliant children exist in most metropolitan areas. Many smaller communities have a Montessori elementary school, which will at least provide a healthy introduction to school for your child. Sometimes parochial schools will permit a child to start kindergarten a year early if a child's birthday is only a few weeks after the state age-cutoff point.

If no possibilities exist for appropriate education or acceleration, parents should attempt to augment the school's paltry fare with supplemental enrichment at home, music lessons, family bull sessions, added reading, and days off from school to pursue educational interests. During this time, you should attempt to uncover other parents of gifted children and work as a group to obtain a school program appropriate for your children.

Talented

No one really knows what a talented child is because there are so many different degrees of talent. But we do know that occasionally we run across a child who has developed one particular skill or talent far beyond his other achievements and far beyond the achievements of age-mates in that area. The talent areas could include almost any field, music, mechanics, writing, art, photography, electronics, gymnastics—whatever. These talent areas have historically been developed outside of the public schools, generally at parent expense for private instruction or by students themselves on a catch-as-catch-can basis. In its recent definition of gifted children, the federal government has included a provision for the "Talented" in this category. Some states which are designing programs for the gifted are also including the talented, partly for the purpose of meeting federal guidelines in order to receive federal funds to subsidize the state programs.

Even though this area is not very well defined and has no objective measurement scales for identifying these persons, parents should know that the category exists. There are children who possess a rare talent which should be nurtured, and not all of these children have parents who are capable of recognizing that talent or financially supporting the training the talent deserves. Parents should check the Talented and Gifted (TAG) programs that might exist in their state or local areas.

Learning-Disabled

Thomas Edison was learning-disabled. So was Albert Einstein, Auguste Rodin, Louis Pasteur, Woodrow Wilson, and a multitude of other geniuses, as well as millions of other persons with average or above average intelligence. And that is how the learning-disabled (LD) child is defined; the Learning Disability category covers a heterogeneous group of children who have average or above average intelligence and who have severe, moderate, or mild learning problems. A child could be simultaneously both gifted and learning-disabled. The LD child is an intelligent child who generally has great difficulties in the public schools.

Until the late 1960s, the LD child was considered the problem child, the child who was labeled either stupid or stubborn, lazy or emotionally disturbed. They are neither stupid nor disturbed. They have good minds, but they learn *differently* from most people. Their minds work differently, sometimes so differently that they ingeniously solve problems that conventional minds cannot solve. Because our schools are so entrenched in the Oatmeal philosophy, school is a disaster for these kids. Only recently, the public schools have begun to make provision for *some* of these kids; but most LD children continue to experience horrendous difficulties in the schools, because most schools make no provision for their "differences," or if they do, the provisions are grossly inadequate and the teaching profession is abysmally ignorant of a true understanding of these children.

How many of these children are there? Many. The statistics vary considerably, but it is estimated that about twenty percent of the U.S. population is learning-disabled. This means that every classroom in America contains at least two or more LD children. Most of them are boys. No one knows why, but there are about five LD boys for every LD girl. This 20-percent figure includes the severe, moderate, and mildly affected children.

No two of them are alike. Because no two of these children are alike in the particular way in which they are "different" and in the degree of "difference," they are very difficult to identify, especially for the ignorant, indifferent teacher who is addicted to Oatmeal and discipline. The constellation of difference is unique to each child. However, research in the last few years has categorized the common characteristics which combine in various ways for each child. An LD child will exhibit one or more of these traits in varying degrees. A few severely affected children will exhibit many or even all of these characteristics, but the severely handicapped child is obvious and generally receives some kind of special attention. It is the moderately or mildly affected LD child, who exhibits only one or two of the characteristics or several of them only to a slight degree, whom the school completely mishandles.

What are the characteristics? The National Advisory Committee on Handicapped Children recently adopted the following definition for these children: " 'Specific learning disability' means ... a disorder in one or more of the basic psychological processes involved in understanding or in using spoken or written language. Such a disorder may be manifested in imperfect ability to listen, think, speak, read, write, spell, or do mathematical calculations. These disorders include such conditions as perceptual handicaps, brain injury, minimal brain dysfunction, dyslexia, developmental aphasia, etc. They do not include learning problems which are due primarily to visual, hearing, or motor handicaps, to mental retardation, emotional disturbance, or to environmental deprivation."

The ten most common characteristics which most authorities attribute to the LD child are as follows:

1. Hyperactivity: constant motion, moving from one object or activity to another. (In some this trait is reversed and there is hypoactivity, slow movement and listlessness.)

2. Perceptual-motor impairments: poor writing, printing, and drawing, deficient eye-hand coordination, problems in throwing or catching a ball, difficulty in reproducing any written image, letters, or numbers.

3. Emotional lability: quick changes of emotional state, cries and laughs easily, with gusto, and shifts from one extreme to another readily.

4. General coordination deficits: may be clumsy or awkward. Gross motor problems cause difficulty in jumping, running, riding a tricycle, etc. Fine motor problems may cause difficulty in buttoning, holding pencils, using dinnerware, etc.

5. Disorders of attention: distractibility or short attention span may be present. The opposite, perseveration, being "locked into" an activity or thought pattern, may also be present. One child may exhibit both extremes of this trait.

6. Impulsiveness: child reacts very quickly to stimuli without thought. This is part of the "now" syndrome attributed to this child. Child may "grab" at objects and people without forethought or self-censure.

7. Memory and thinking disorders: child may have long- and short-term memory deficits. He may also experience problems in processing or integrating thoughts or skills.

8. Specific academic deficits: The child may encounter difficulty with one or more academic areas, such as arithmetic, reading, writing, spelling, or language.

9. Dysfunction of hearing and speech: Although his hearing is normal, he is unable to receive and to process auditory input. He may have difficulty understanding and using expressive language.

10. Equivocal neurological signs: "soft" neurological signs, such as mixed and/or confusion of laterality, poor coordination of ocular muscles, poor finger coordination, and general awkwardness. Child may have a "borderline" or abnormal electroencephalogram (brain wave recording).

What causes this? There is no one single cause. Sometimes brain damage from an accident, birth, or fever can cause it; but this is not true in all cases. For some, the cause is simply a developmental lag; some of these children will outgrow the organic problems, but not the psychological and academic damage done in the meantime. Research also indicates that genetic factors are the basis for the irregularity. Cases have also been built for diet and body-chemistry deficiencies as causes. A great deal of literature exists on this subject which will not be explored here. While the causes may be interesting, the problem of educating these children is of much more importance. And we *can* do something about the education of these children, whereas it may be many years before we know enough to ameliorate the causes.

What can be done about educating them? Ideally, an LD child should be recognized as such prior to attaining school age; and his specific deficits should be treated by specialized educational remediation to prepare the child for the "regular" kindergarten. Much can be done to help these children compensate for their "differences" at an early age. Research has shown that the earlier a child receives specialized education, the better the child's chances of adapting to the world of learning. However, this early identification is difficult, both clinically and logistically. Children with only mild or moderate problems often do not exhibit LD traits until they begin formal schooling. Unfortunately, most of them are not identified until about second grade, after they have experienced a great deal of failure. By this time, the child has generally developed a decided aversion to school and the ignorant educators have labeled the child as "bad." In most cases, that is where this child remains for the rest of his school days—until he drops out or is thrown out of the schools.

Special education programs and specially trained LD teachers are available to a few of these children in *some* of the schools. The rest, the large majority of LD children, receive no special help. They are at the mercy of teachers oriented to "Oatmeal and discipline" who either have no knowledge of the learning styles of these children or who reject the research on the basis of their over-inflated personal opinion which cannot be confused by facts.

Some states have laws which mandate specialized education for all identified LD children, and this list of states is growing every year. Even in states which mandate education for these children, many children are deprived of appropriate education because they have not been *identified* as needing it. Specialized programs including specialized staff cost money. School systems which wish to limit the costs of specialized education do so by

merely refusing to identify very many LD·children. Identification is difficult under the best of circumstances and
next to impossible if the school system has a need to limit
its expenditures. School psychologists and teachers are
told how many children the system can afford to accommodate, never mind the number of children who need
help. This topic, however, is treated in the chapter "Hot-
Air Balloons" under the problems of professionals.

*If I suspect my child may have a learning disability,
how can I get help for him?* You better find out what you
are dealing with before you make any move in terms of
the school. First, you should begin serious study of some
of the many books written on this highly complex subject. Good starter books are *Something's Wrong With My
Child* by Milton Brutten, Sylvia Richardson, and Charles
Mangel, and *Educational Handicap, a Handbook for
Teachers and Parents* by Alice Thompson. Later you can
get into more sophisticated, research-oriented works.
Next, find out if your community or one nearby has a
chapter of the Association for Children with Learning
Disabilities (ACLD). This national organization of parents and LD specialists has monthly meetings in communities throughout the nation, and it is a *must* for all
parents of LD children. This organization is devoted to
dispensing information and aiding parents in obtaining
help for their LD child. If you cannot find information
about this organization locally, write the National Office
of ACLD at 5225 Grace Street, Pittsburgh, Pennsylvania,
15236, for information.

Through personal discussions with the highly informed members of ACLD, obtain the names of competent, private educational consultants whom you can contact for an impartial diagnostic assessment of your child.
Do not, repeat, *do not,* ask your local school psychologist
for this assessment until you have first become informed
about his qualifications and the local school system's poli-

tics through ACLD members. If you live in an isolated area which does not have an ACLD chapter, contact your state ACLD president who will give you the information you need.

Many school psychologists as well as many psychologists in private practice have no real knowledge of learning disabilities; the field is too new, especially for those who received their training before the 1960s and for those who attended schools without faculty trained in this field. All psychologists pretend to understand learning disabilities because they have heard the term and naturally wish to exploit the field to their own personal advantage. Don't get caught in this futile, time-wasting trap.

After you have obtained a thorough evaluation of your child (this could be several months after you begin your search), you can begin your pursuit of a suitable education for your child. Again, the best source of unbiased information about schools, programs, and teachers is the ACLD. If you have obtained a competent consultant-advocate through them, you will have by this time become quite knowledgeable concerning educational programs. It is at this point that your battle begins.

If a competent psychologist has diagnosed your child as LD and has made educational recommendations to you, your job for the next few years is to become an expert on your child's specific deficits and needs. You will have to become the authority and supervisor of his education because there will be constant changes in the school, the programs, the teachers, and your child's needs, even in the best circumstances. You will need to monitor his education as a watchdog guards his master's home.

It is impossible to anticipate the multitudinous circumstances any parent might encounter in seeking suitable education for a learning-disabled child. If your state has a law mandating education for the learning-disabled, you have a good chance of obtaining it—but only if you fight for it and know your child's specific needs better than any other person. With a state mandate, you can use Parental Persistence to obtain an appropriate specialist to instruct your child, even if it means having your child transported to a different school system each day to receive it. Should your school system not provide specialized help from *qualified* personnel, you should use Parental Persistence at the level of the department of public instruction to obtain it for your child. This can be done and has been done by parents who have been willing to fight for their children's rights to an education. "Gotcha Games" and "Hot-Air Balloons" are chapters which are also helpful to parents of LD children.

What can I do if my state does not mandate specialized education for my LD child? The federal government has established special education agencies with offices and staff in many communities throughout the nation. The purpose of this program for handicapped children is to provide suitable education for all children needing it whose local school does not provide for them. These offices use a variety of names in the various states in which the program operates. Information on this program can be obtained by writing to the U.S. Office of Education in Washington, D.C.

You should also assess the private schools and even parochial schools in your area. One of them might be a better place for your child than your local public school. If there is a major university near you, talk with faculty members of the special education department because some of these schools operate clinics under the university's auspices.

It would be a good idea to join the ACLD groups in your state who are seeking some of the same answers you are. A state mandate is one of the goals of that group, you can be sure. But, of course, in the meantime you will want to do anything you can to help your child, because legislation often takes years in the making. By 1980, the new federal law PL 94-142, should make available services in all districts—if you demand them.

You might be able to locate "alternative" or "drop-in" schools in your area for junior-high and high-school-age children. These probably are not designed specifically for LD children, but sometimes they are more appropriate than a regular school.

Another possibility would be for the parents of several LD children to hire an unemployed teacher to privately teach their children. In essence this would be creating a private school. If you can afford to do this and know four to ten other LD children whose parents would join you, this could be a solution, especially for elementary-age children. There are many unemployed teachers who would be willing to take a few special education courses in summer school if they were assured of a job for the next year. Since education for LD children must be individualized, an age-mix of children would be no problem. The school session could be for less than a full-time day, perhaps from nine until one. This type of child should not be subjected to full-time school days. A family's basement or family room could serve very well as a classroom for four to ten children. This would cost very little more than tuition at a private parochial school.

If you were to decide to take this course of action, don't be afraid to violate your state's school attendance laws. Parents all over the country are doing this kind of thing, and many for religious reasons and other reasons far less important than the needs of exceptional children. State departments of public instruction are quite reluctant to exert pressure on parents who take their children out of the schools, because the resultant publicity is bad for the schools. Many states permit this under the condition that a certified teacher is tutoring the child. Action of this sort by parents is often the impetus needed to obtain school reforms and appropriate education through the public institutions. It might even be a good idea to appeal to the federal Office of Education for financial help in designing this alternative schooling.

There are excellent private, residential schools for exceptional children located in several areas of the nation, but these are exceedingly expensive for the average family, with fees running from eight to fifteen thousand dollars per year. For those few who can afford this price and are willing to send their child away to school, these schools are highly successful.

Whatever course you should decide to take, no solution will be permanent, and you will have to keep very close tabs on your child's progress and constantly changing needs. After all, you parents are the only persons who are totally concerned for and dedicated to the welfare of your child.

Emotionally Disturbed, Behaviorally Disordered, and Socially Maladjusted

These terms are all negative and all "scarey," and they are labels that are often capriciously and erroneously attached to children. The term "emotionally disturbed" is most often attached to the withdrawn child who doesn't do the assignments. The term "behaviorally disordered" is most often attached to the child who does things that annoy the teacher. The term "socially maladjusted" is usually applied only to those children who actually fight with other children, because most teachers have little concern for those children who are merely miserable. In all three cases, the disturbance is attributed to a variety of problems in the home or the neighborhood. As you may well guess from having read the information on the learning-disabled children, many of these children because of their emotional lability, impulsiveness and poor self-concept resulting from school failure, will be seen by teachers as fitting into one of these categories. Some school systems and most teachers make no differentiation

between these categories, but lump them all together under the general category of emotionally disturbed. Here is
a typical checklist given by some school systems to their
teachers to help them diagnose your child:

A TEACHER'S CHECKLIST
FOR DETECTING EMOTIONAL DISTURBANCE

If the answer to any of the following questions is
"yes," then the teacher should refer the parents to
some source where the child and the parents can be
evaluated and possibly treated. The school can then
send its report to the referral agency, using this
checklist as a guide, and including the teacher's
comments. This action will expedite diagnosis and
treatment, and it may even prevent further development of the problem and other undetected problems.

A. Disturbed Attitudes toward Self:
1. Has an inflated sense of adequacy and exhibits an unrealistic view of his abilities. Feels he is
privileged and does not have to do what he does not
want to do, even when confronted with the truth
by others.
2. Feels inferior, seeing himself as not possessing the ability to do the things he can do. Criticizes
himself and may even express the wish that he were
dead.
3. Sees himself as bad, feeling that his desires,
feelings and impulses are sinful. Indicates that he
needs to be punished even when others do not think
punishment is needed.
4. Feels that he cannot love anyone or be nice
to anyone.
5. Has problems with guilt, both positive and
negative. Feels guilty when he should not, or he
does not feel guilty when he should.
6. Has sex-identity confusion. Identifies with
sex other than his/her own. Displays interests normally associated with opposite sex.
7. Views some part of his body as ugly or even
freakish.
8. Sees himself as mentally retarded or crazy.
May call himself names to that effect.

B. Disturbing Classroom Behaviors:
   1. Asks to go to the restroom excessively.
   2. Short attention span, cannot concentrate. Does not finish assigned tasks.
   3. Seeks attention, exhibitionistic. Shows off.
   4. Daydreams excessively. Is not interested in school.
   5. Destructive. Breaks things, mishandles, kicks, bumps into desks, etc.
   6. Extremely impulsive. Doesn't think things through before acting; instant reaction to stimuli.
   7. Cannot tolerate frustration. Doesn't wait his turn, seeks immediate rewards.
   8. Will not or cannot follow rules. Does not accept restraints or limits.
   9. Rigidity. Must follow own precise way of doing things. Tries to fix things he insists are misplaced or need straightening.
   10. Ritualistic. Taps teacher's desk three times each time he approaches it.
   11. Resists changing to new activities. Wants to work at one task to exclusion of all others.
   12. Perseverates in annoying purposeless behaviors. Makes obnoxious sounds with mouth and tongue, taps pencils on desk or kicks desk, swings feet or waves arms.
   13. Indecisive and doubtful. Does not accept responsibility for making decisions.
   14. Fearful or apprehensive. Sometimes depressed or moody.
   15. Will deny he misbehaved, even when he is caught "red-handed."
   16. Excessively impatient for lunch time to come.

C. Disturbed Behavior Toward Teacher:
   1. Gets his feelings hurt easily. Cannot accept criticism.
   2. Excessively shy with teacher and other adults who confront him.
   3. Overly dependent on teacher. Asks many questions in over-concern with pleasing teacher.
   4. Demands too much of teacher's time. Tries to monopolize teacher.
   5. Overly aggressive. Resists teacher's requests

or suggestions, stubbornly following his own methods or plans.

6. Hypercritical. Says class activities are "dumb" or teacher is "unfair."

7. Steals from teacher. Takes pencils etc. without asking.

D. Disturbances with Peers:

1. Aggressive and hostile. Acts as a bully. Gets out of seat to interact with others, talking, teasing or fighting.

2. Fearful and shy with others. Withdrawn.

3. Excessively competitive with others. Wants to be first and best.

4. Tattles on others, expecting teacher to handle his problems.

5. Used as a scapegoat by classmates.

6. Brags and boasts. Talks excessively about his personal possessions and family activities.

E. Sexual Disturbances:

1. Masturbates, either overtly or covertly.

2. Uses "dirty" words, swears and curses.

3. Genital oriented. Touches or hits genitals or buttocks of classmates.

4. Asks questions of sexual nature frequently; overly concerned about birth process.

5. Goes to restroom excessively.

F. Speech Disturbances:

1. Discretionary mutism. Refuses to speak at school, but parents insist that child speaks with them.

2. Extremely fearful when speaking before others. Speaks too softly to be heard. Stammers or stutters.

3. Uses baby talk. Speech inappropriate to child's age.

4. Speaks too loudly, demanding attention and control.

G. Infantile Behavior:

1. Resists separation from parent. Says he wants to go home. Cries for parent.

2. Temper tantrums. Lies on floor, kicks and screams.

3. Sucks thumb or fingers.
4. Unable or unwilling to dress himself, i.e., buttoning coat, tying shoes.

H. Physical Disturbances:
1. Bites or picks fingernails.
2. Vomits in class frequently.
3. Bad breath.
4. Chronically fatigued. Tired or listless.
5. Tics. Facial twitches. Involuntary blinking of eyes.
6. Obesity or emaciation with no organic origin.
7. Skin eruptions. Picks at sores and scabs. Scratches itches.
8. Body odor.

I. Learning Problems:
1. Discrepancy in abilities in different types of classroom tasks, e.g., being good in arithmetic, but poor in reading, or vice versa.
2. Discrepancy between IQ or achievement test scores and the level of performance in class.

Biased by this kind of teacher input, a school psychologist often will rubber-stamp the teacher-diagnosis for the variety of reasons explained in "Hot-Air Balloons." No one but the psychologist on the school staff is qualified to diagnose any child as disturbed or maladjusted. While it is true that there are disturbed and maladjusted children in our society, this kind of label is often used as a blame-placing tactic by the school to explain away its own inadequacies. If a child is truly disturbed or maladjusted, parents will experience manifestations of that disturbance at home. But since most or all of the undesirable behavior occurs at school, the child may well be suffering from school-phobia or outraged indignation with the school's miserable treatment of him.

Even if a child has a bad home situation, the school cannot change the home, and sociologists meddling via home visits usually do not help a child. Should the home be a bad scene, it is even more important for the school to compensate and provide a warm, human, self-concept-

building environment to help the child become a worthwhile, self-respecting member of the community. Attaching a derogatory label to the child does not accomplish
this.

The school should "clean up its own house" before
criticizing the homes of children. Maladjusted academic
instruction and maladjusted teacher-behavior which lead
a child to failure and a sense of personal worthlessness
are the major causes of student misbehavior. Anyone
who has any spirit and who has not been whipped into
cowed submission erupts occasionally when his environment becomes intolerable. The school produces the environment which provokes the student behavior to which
the school objects. It is not the child, but the school which
is maladjusted.

*What can I do if the school suggests or assigns one
of these labels to my child?* Do not accept it: Use Parental
Persistence to obtain more appropriate academic instruction and respectful teacher-behavior for your child. Frequent bases for assigning these labels is a child's refusal
to do schoolwork assigned to him or his apparent "disrespect" for the teacher. To wit:

> Ms. DEE RESPECT: Mr. Parent, we called this con-
> ference to try to help Johnnie. I'm sure you know
> that things have not been going well, and we have
> all been working very hard to find a solution. We
> think Johnnie's problem is a very deep-seated one
> and beyond our ability to handle as ordinary class-
> room teachers. [Notice the irony: her expressed
> modesty in dealing with Johnnie on one side and
> yet her audacity for diagnosing him on the other
> side.]
>
> YOU: I don't understand what you are trying to
> say. I would like you to be more explicit.
>
> Ms. DEE RESPECT: [Encouraged and warming to

her subject.] Well, Johnnie doesn't do his work the way he should. He just sits and stares out the window when he is supposed to be working on his programmed reading book, his arithmetic book, and other assignments, and when I've tried to encourage him to get to work, he is most rude and disrespectful. Just the other day, he told me to "Butt out and buzz off!"

YOU: Yes, he told me about that. He said that you were very angry and came over to him and said, "You lazy good-for-nothing lout, you get busy— right now." If someone approached me with that kind of "encouragement" I think I would probably tell him to butt out and buzz off, or even something much worse.

MS. DEE RESPECT: [Indignant.] Well, I said nothing of the sort. [Well, now you know what you are dealing with. Treat it accordingly.]

MR. SI CHOLOGIST: [Very dignified and bed-side-mannerish.] Mr. Parent, Ms. Respect has asked me in to observe Johnnie several times, and through extensive consultation with her and through my own observations of Johnnie, I think we are dealing with a very serious problem, and I would like to talk to Johnnie and run him through some tests to see if we can come up with some good, positive solutions. [Notice how he ignored Ms. Respect's misbehavior and is trying to divert you with a "serious problem." He has already revealed his bias toward Johnnie via the "extensive consultations" and his negative observations. There is no way his tests could be objective. He has already revealed his diagnosis without any talking with Johnnie, let alone testing him.]

YOU: What tests would you plan to use? [This question is not necessary since he revealed himself, but if he has remained silent about his orientation, you might want to know something about it.]

MR. SI CHOLOGIST: I'm not sure, just yet, but I like to use the Rorschach, the Kinetic Family Drawing Test, and the Sentence Completion Test. And naturally, I'll give him an intelligence test, probably the Wechsler WISC. [Except for the WISC, these are all projective tests, which, with his obvious bias, will prove Ms. Dee Respect's diagnosis. Don't permit it.]

YOU: No, I don't think that is necessary. We have no problem with Johnnie at home, and your testing would not help his school situation, which is where *you* are having problems. Rather, I want Ms. Respect to learn to control her anger and her abusive language with Johnnie, and I want her to try to find a more stimulating way of teaching him. He is an intelligent boy, who finds school terribly boring.

MS. RESPECT: But Mr. Parent, if you will not cooperate with us, we cannot help Johnnie. [Now it is your fault—you're "uncooperative." This is a guilt hook.] And we simply cannot put up with Johnnie's lack of respect. [This is a threat to you. Notice how the school accepts no responsibility for its inadequacies.]

YOU: I want you to treat Johnnie with respect and then he will treat you with respect. Respect is a two-way street, and respect is earned, not demanded. [You have returned the conversation to Ms. Respect's inadequacies which they are trying very hard to ignore.]

MR. SI CHOLOGIST: How does Johnnie behave at

home? Does he give you the respect he should? [Back to blaming you for their problems!]

YOU: We give Johnnie the respect he should have as a human being and a full member of the family, and he returns that respect. I want you people to accord him the respect every child should have.

MS. DEE RESPECT: But there is a difference between children and adults. Children cannot be in control. If we did that, we would have chaos here. [She has shown her ignorance. She equates giving human respect with giving control.]

YOU: You evidently don't understand the word respect. We control Johnnie with reason, not authority. This is a difference which you should understand. When adults behave irrationally and control through authority alone, then they offend the child's intelligence and self-respect. An adult has to behave as a mature, rational person in order to earn a child's respect. I want you, Ms. Respect, to behave that way toward Johnnie. You'll be surprised at how well it will work. Will you try it?

MS. DEE RESPECT: [Resignedly.] Of course, but ... [She shrugs to suggest futility.]

YOU: Good. I'll talk with Johnnie and tell him that you are willing to cooperate and that we want him to do the same. And my wife and I will be following very closely how things go from here. We'll be visiting school, talking with your principal, and I hope that, Mr. Chologist, you will be observing teacher-behavior as well as student-behavior.

This may not be the end of the problem. If not, the school will at this point begin one of the "Gotcha Games" to protect Ms. Dee Respect's investment in her own opinion. If Johnnie's school situation does not improve, you may want to demand a different teacher for him, one who is more intelligent, more creative, and one who is not prejudiced toward Johnnie. But at least you have refused to allow the school to stigmatize Johnnie with an "undesirable" label which could haunt him for the rest of his life, and all for no reason except a teacher's inadequacies.

Slow Learners and Retarded

Depending upon individual cases, slow learners achieve below their capability if placed in special classes for the retarded. However, if the student has a poor self-concept, he may be benefitted by placement with the educable mentally retarded.

Most schools now provide special classes for the educable mentally retarded. With proper educational opportunity, these students can attain minimum skills in reading and mathematics and writing so that they can obtain jobs such as janitor, waitress, and cook, and can obtain additional training for factory and business positions. Many of these students are well adjusted and retarded only in academic pursuits. Unfortunately, a disproportionate number of students placed in this category nationally are the culturally different who get low scores on tests designed for and administered by middle-class people.

Trainable mentally retarded young people are entitled to educational opportunity. As the schools accept their responsibility to offer education to them, the trend away from institutionalization may grow. It is cheaper tax-wise for the public to assume its responsibility to these citizens at the local level than to continually enlarge the state institutions. With appropriate educational help and family devotion, most of these citizens can learn to take personal care of themselves as well as many housekeeping skills. The goal of education is development of the individual to his capacity. We as a society owe this to these individuals as much as to the gifted.

7

Parents' Guide to School Records and Test Scores

The federal Right to Privacy law recently enacted gives parents the right to read their child's school record, challenge the contents if they choose, and to seek expungement or correction of false information contained in that permanent record. This right belongs to parents of students under the age of eighteen and to the student himself if he is over the age of eighteen. In some states, students have the right of access to their records at an earlier age. In order to properly exercise this long overdue right, parents should have some knowledge about some of the tests for which they will find test scores in the school's permanent records.

Many people don't know one type of test from another, let alone the differences between the myriad of tests within each category. But parents should not feel reluctant to attempt an understanding of these scores because of this. If parents understand the contents of the next few pages, which give simple nontechnical explanations of these tests, they will know as much about tests as many teachers.

On the basis of very limited knowledge, teachers read the files and make crucial decisions about Johnnie's future. Parents are entitled to at least the same prerogative. As a group, with few exceptions, teachers are appallingly ignorant about test scores and what they mean. College students preparing to be teachers find test information difficult to grasp; they retain an understanding of the material only through the completion of the examination, or they refuse to learn it because they "do not believe" in tests. So fear not parents! Your very fundamental knowledge of tests might disclose that Johnnie's teachers are in actuality abusing test scores.

In our dealings with teachers, we have observed a rather strange, ambivalent attitude toward tests. If test scores for a student happen to coincide with or support a teacher's personal opinion of a student, that teacher touts those test scores as though they were infallible. But if that same teacher encounters tests scores which are contrary to her personal opinion of a particular student, she will declare flatly that "test scores don't mean anything," and will proceed to ignore them and act accordingly. This schizophrenic approach to tests is a glorious example of cognitive dissonance, a concept to which all teachers should have been exposed in their training; in effect, it leads to the learning or acceptance of only those things which are in agreement with previous experience and beliefs—or prejudices.

Do test scores mean anything? Generally speaking, yes. The good tests, the ones which have been highly researched and highly tested themselves, have proven to be pretty good *indications* of whatever factor they are measuring. Many test scores are valid and reliable for the vast majority of the persons who take them. But no one test score is proof of anything; for some rare individuals, no amount of testing would adequately describe that person. There are many variables and aspects of testing that advise even the most knowledgeable person to take test scores with a grain of salt.

Tests given in groups are not valid for a small portion of the population. This group includes those for whom English is not the native language, those who have reading deficiencies, those whose physical or emotional health is not functioning at normal levels on the day the test is taken, those whose motivation is so low that they don't take the test seriously, and those who have neurological problems which, if properly diagnosed, would place them in special education programs. It is for these reasons that no one test score is proof of anything and that tests should be interpreted by skilled persons whose discriminating judgment recognizes the limitations of tests.

Tests are not infallible. Nor is the surgeon's knife infallible. But we don't throw away the scalpel because it does not always achieve perfection. There are many variables which limit the success of surgery. Some conditions do not call for surgery and some do not respond to surgery. Sometimes the surgeon makes a mistake. Yet we all believe in surgery and consider it a boon to man. But we certainly would not trust a nurse's aide to use surgery to cut us open. Many teachers are no more prepared to use psychological tests than the nurse's aide is prepared to perform an apendectomy.

There are those people who object to the very existence of IQ tests. This objection comes from individuals and groups of individuals whose IQ scores are not as high as they would like them to be. Probably the major cause of this furor is that all tests are based on what is *average*. To establish what is normal or average, we take the point at which half the population scores above and half scores below. In so doing, half of the population must be below average—and who wants to be below average? The very act of setting up a normal average automatically offends half of the people. It is often those who score below their desired self-image who attack the tests and declare the tests inferior.

The basis for denouncing IQ tests is the wishful thinking that all men are created equal—in terms of intelligence. Nature is not democratic, despite wishes to the contrary. Not everyone can be "above average"; it is a contradiction of terms. Those persons who deny the influence of heredity on intelligence and write off all variation of intelligence to differences in environment, especially blaming lack of money for low intelligence, are unrealistic.

While it is true that environment plays a considerable role in the development of potential, it does not create the potential. The very best of environments can develop a potential only up to its limits—wherever nature established it. A poor environment can inhibit the development of intellectual potential, but except in cases of severe organic damage, it does not really decrease the potential. The potential is always there, whether it is developed or not developed. Everyone has known persons who did not do well in school but yet achieved great success in later years. This person's potential was not developed by the schools, but the person managed to develop at least part of his potential despite the schools.

The better intelligence tests are based on thorough research and have high validity and high reliability. The validity of IQ tests is based on abilities our civilization considers important, the ability to learn to read, to do mathematics, to use language, to understand science, to understand ideas, to solve problems, to create—to perform tasks which are considered essential to building and improving our civilization. IQ tests correlate extremely well with those abilities. Our civilization calls these abilities intelligence. While these abilities may not be the whole of intelligence, they are what our civilization has scientifically identified up to this point. If we were to deny these abilities as intelligence, we would be denying our civilization, our science, our communication systems, our industry and technology, our arts—all of civilization as we know it. Intelligence tests are valid for our civilization. As our civilization advances, in the humanities, sciences, and technology, we may assume that intelligence tests will also advance and improve as they have for the last seventy years.

Reliability of IQ tests has been statistically substantiated through much research over a period of many years. The question of reliability, "Does this test do its job of measuring consistently," has been answered yes by the research. Anyone who has worked with school records knows this is true for the vast majority; the several IQ scores for any one student are within a few points of each other with few exceptions. Only in rare cases do several tests indicate significant contradictions. Counselors and psychologists are supposed to be trained to understand this and deal with it appropriately.

Critics of IQ tests talk a great deal about the self-fulfilling prophecy as their chief argument against IQ tests. The tendency to become what we believe we are, or, by extension, what we are taught to believe we are, is a truth we are all aware of. But abolishing the use of IQ tests would create a much more capricious and prejudicial system for judging ability or intelligence. Without tests, the subjective *opinion* of educators would determine who is intelligent and who is not. With this kind of nonobjective, nonscientific, non-researched system, many more children would suffer through erroneous categorizing and the consequential negative self-fulfilling prophecy. I would rather have my child's abilities judged scientifically by a highly researched, objective, unemotional, unprejudiced test than to be judged by the emotional whimsy of human opinion.

When seeing group tests scores, parents should look for patterns of consistency, if the child is old enough to have been tested more than once. If several tests of any one factor, such as intelligence, tend to be consistent, that is, varying no more than a few points, then the test score is probably a pretty good indication of that ability, assuming, of course, that the child does not fall into that small group for whom tests are neither valid nor reliable.

Probably the most common error the layman makes when looking at test scores is to assume that all tests are tests of ability or intelligence. This is not true, but it is a misconception that the schools have done very little to dispel—probably because so many educators do not really understand the difference themselves. Schools use several varieties of tests for different purposes. In addition to tests of intelligence, schools use achievement tests, aptitude tests, interest tests, and occasionally personality tests.

What is an intelligence test? Intelligence tests attempt to measure a person's innate intellectual potential, or ability to learn. Research on intelligence tests goes back to before the turn of the century to the work of Alfred Binet whose work culminated in a revision which we know today as the Stanford-Binet intelligence test. This granddaddy of intelligence tests spawned research into intelligence that surpasses research on all other types of tests. Study of intelligence has been like research in any scientific field in that the more that is learned about the subject, the more we realize how little we know. There are hundreds of intelligence tests in existence; some of them are very good tests and some of them are not worth the paper on which they are printed.

There are two basic types of intelligence tests, individual tests and group tests. Most people, including most school children, have never taken an individual test. But everyone has taken a group test and has the scores in his permanent school record. A group test is a paper-and-pencil test given to large groups at the same time. Widely used group tests include the Kuhlmann-Anderson tests, the Otis Quick-Scoring Mental Ability Tests, the Lorge-Thorndike Intelligence Tests, the Henmon-Nelson Tests of Mental Ability, and the California Test of Mental Maturity.

The two individual intelligence tests commonly given to children are the Stanford-Binet and the Weschler Intelligence Scale for Children, the latter commonly referred to as the WISC. The Wechsler Adult Intelligence Scale (WAIS) is given to children over the age of fifteen. In all probability, your child has not taken an individual test unless he has had serious school problems. These individual tests are administered only by specially trained persons, generally a school psychologist or a counselor. The test, which takes approximately two hours, is given on a one-to-one basis, with the examiner "talking" the child through the test.

The individual intelligence test is the best kind of intelligence test; the validity and reliability is higher than for any group test. Because of the personalized method of the administration, this test has value for even a good portion of those whom the group test does not adequately measure. The individual test will identify language problems, reading problems, motivation problems, and will give clues to some emotional and neurological problems.

Intelligence is not a single entity. We all have many intelligences, even though all intelligence tests give a single-number score as though there were a single intelligence. This is one of the basic differences between a "good" intelligence test and a "poor" one. The better tests measure several of these intelligences and give scores for each of them; when these scores are combined, they give that single IQ score with which everyone is familiar.

What are these intelligences? There is no real agreement as to what these are or how many there are. Lewis Terman, one of the American pioneers in intelligence testing, designed the American version of the Stanford-Binet to measure one general intelligence, which has been described as the ability to deal with abstractions. At the other extreme, J. P. Guilford suggested a multi-intelligence theory which divided intelligence into 120 components. Obviously, there are several intelligences, even though controversy exists as to how many. But most intelligence tests deal with the following factors:

Verbal reasoning—knowledge of words and ability to use them.

Numerical reasoning—ability to understand and use number concepts.

Abstract reasoning—ability to think symbolically, to deal with ideas as opposed to concrete examples.

Spacial reasoning—ability to form and deal with concepts of space, i.e., mentally reversing a house floor-plan or a pattern.

Memory—ability to retain information, both short-range and long-range.

The single, composite IQ score in a school record is not nearly as important for planning appropriate education for children as the various subscores which make up the composite. It is helpful to those who wish to help a child to know where specifically the child's strengths and weaknesses lie. The separate subscores for the various abilities will vary from each other somewhat for all persons, but they tend to "hang together." In other words, a person who has superior verbal ability will have at least average or above average numerical ability. A small difference between two abilities can be greatly magnified by interest and experience over the years. This magnification accounts for the apparent ability differences we all see in ourselves.

For a few people, these subscores do not "hang together," especially for children with school problems. In other words, some abilities may be quite high while others are quite low. This kind of "scatter" is a good indication that further testing should be done to determine whether or not special education is needed. If your child is experiencing problems, a look at the subscores of an individual test to find strengths and weaknesses would be advised, in order to teach to the strengths and to the weaknesses.

OK, but what do the numbers mean? If the number is given in terms of an IQ score, it depends somewhat on the test because some tests tend to give higher scores than others. A few points one way or the other should not be taken seriously due to variance of tests and "chance error." Generally speaking, IQ scores can be converted this way:

		Percent of population
130 and above	— Gifted range	2
115 — 130	— Superior range	14
85 — 115	— Normal range	68
70 — 85	— Slow learner	14
below 70	— Retarded	2

Probably the greatest problem area is within the normal range. This category runs from borderline-retarded to borderline-superior. Unfortunately, the schools tend to teach all these children the same way, using the Oatmeal philosophy discussed earlier. To make matters worse, in many schools, those in the slow-learner category are also fed Oatmeal. This is a place where parents must make sure teaching is adjusted to the child's individual needs.

Percentiles is the system used for reporting most test scores other than intelligence test scores. It is a simple system to understand because everyone has a basic understanding of percentages on which it is based. Most test publishers provide percentile conversion charts for their tests, and this system is the one most commonly used by the schools. A percentile is a comparison score which simply states where a person ranks in every hundred per-

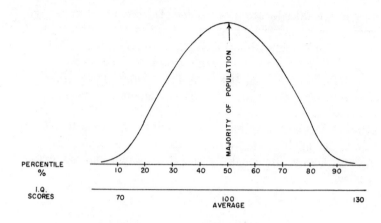

Figure 7-1   I.Q. and percentile scores compared

sons taking the test. For example, if your child's percentile score is 80, this means that out of every hundred children taking the test, your child did better than 80 and not as well as 20. A score of 50 is average; a few points one way or the other are not important.

In using percentiles, however, care must be taken to find out what group has been used for the comparison. Some schools have a nasty habit of juggling comparison groups in an effort to make their school look good. You should find out if the percentile "norms" used for reporting compares Johnnie with only the other kids in his school, or compares him with all the kids his age in the city, state or in the nation. Sometimes schools with low academic standards will refrain from using comparison groups that make the school look bad.

What are achievement tests? Achievement tests are simply a measure of what a person has learned. Achievement tests are *not* a measure of ability. An achievement test is the best test for measuring how well a teacher or school is performing; it is the best test of a "good" teacher from an academic standpoint.

Naturally, what one learns depends partly on his ability to learn—on his intelligence. But our schools are standardized to the point that all children in the normal range of intelligence should be achieving "at grade level." A child of normal intelligence should not be achieving two or three grades behind his grade level. When there is a discrepancy between the intelligence score and the achievement score—when a child is not achieving up to his potential—the school is at fault and should devise alternate teaching methods to pull the child up to where he belongs. In short, the school should find a substitute for Oatmeal for this child in the particular subject with which he is having difficulty.

In the elementary grades, achievement tests measure accomplishment primarily in reading and arithmetic. Some of the achievement tests used by schools are the Iowa Basic Skills test battery, The Metropolitan Achievement test battery, Wide Range Achievement Tests, and many separate tests, both group and individual, for measuring achievement in specific areas.

Achievement tests measure how well the school is doing, certainly as much as, if not more than, how well Johnnie is doing. If Suzie's verbal IQ score is average or higher, her reading achievement scores should be average or higher. If the reading achievement is low, then there is something the school is not doing correctly. It is your job as a parent to make sure that the school finds a better way to teach reading to Suzie.

When inspecting achievement test scores particularly, it is important to find out what "norms" or comparison the school is using. If the school tells you that Suzie has an arithmetic achievement at the 50th percentile level, find out if that means 50th percentile nationally, statewide, or locally. It is in the area of achievement that schools tend to "juggle" the comparison scales in order to make the school look good and keep the parents off their backs. This is especially true in the last few years as achievement scores nationally have been falling, hitting a new low each year for the last twelve years. This means that the schools have been teaching less and less each year for the last twelve years.

Big-city averages are lower than the national average. Suburban averages run from the national average to considerably higher. Small-school scores run higher than large-school averages. Recently, rural-area scores have begun to run higher than urban-area averages, with some exceptions both ways. State averages vary considerably; some state averages are very high and some are very low when compared to each other as they are in the national averages. Private-school averages are higher than public-school averages. Some affluent schools which should be producing above national norms are not; parents should seek answers for this.

A variety of achievement tests are used at the junior-high and high-school level. These tests measure accomplishment in the areas of math, English, social studies, science, and generally give a composite score. Again, these tests measure how well the school does in teaching knowledge in these subject areas to each particular child.

What are interest tests? Just what the title indicates —interest. These tests are normally not given until junior high school and after because interest has not jelled until then. But parents should understand that high interest does not necessarily mean high ability in the same area. While it is true that we all are interested in those things at which we excel, at the same time, we all excel at different ability levels. A student whose highest interest is in science is not necessarily destined to become a physicist or a physician. If he has high intelligence, high achievement in math and science, and high interest in sci-

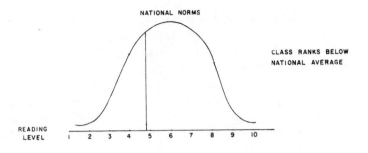

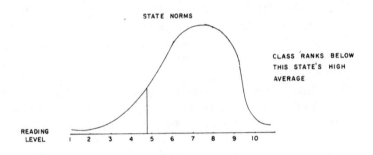

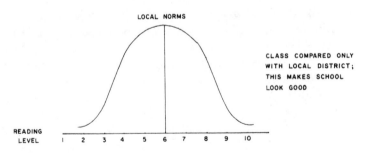

Figure 7-2   Comparison of reading achievement norms
for the same 6th-grade class

ence, then Johnnie stands a pretty good chance of becoming a scientist. If Johnnie were to have high interest in

science, with average intelligence and achievement, the
chances are that Johnnie would be a good candidate for
a science-related position, such as a technician in a lab-
oratory or a salesman of science products.

Many other human factors must be considered when
making career decisions. Personality, drive, ambition, and
opportunity are among these. Interest tests, like most
tests, can give clues for planning, but they are not the
whole story.

Research has shown that basic interests do not change
much from the age of sixteen through adulthood. Therefore, interest tests have considerable reliability, but their
validity can be thrown way off base if the person taking
the test is not completely honest. In other words, interest
tests can be "loaded" to come out any way a person wants
because these tests are "self-report" answer-oriented.
Sometimes a "halo" effect registers on an interest test
when a young person admires someone in a particular profession. That profession is then viewed romantically by
the student.

The two best interest tests are the Kuder Preference
Test and the Strong Vocational Interest Blank. The Kuder
is the most commonly used in schools.

What about personality tests? No parent should ever
willingly permit his child to take a personality test of any
sort. The test instruments themselves have never been
proven by research to be valid or reliable, and they are,
at best, controversial among the people who know the
most about them. Personality tests are the weakest of all
tests from the standpoint of objectivity.

A personality test can do your child no good, but it
might do him a good deal of harm. Personality tests are
used by schools primarily to pin derogatory labels on kids.
These labels do not help the child, but they do give the
school excuses for not educating that child. The best
"score" one can obtain on a personality test is that of

"normal." The worst "score" can be any number of mental-aberration labels. Parents should insist that the school assume that a child is emotionally normal.

The schools are in the business of educating, not the business of providing psychotherapy. Therefore, there can be no positive, educational help for a child who is diagnosed by the school as emotionally disturbed. If you do feel that there is a chance that your child might have emotional problems, seek the opinion of a competent psychiatrist, psychologist or counselor who is in no way connected with the school system.

There are multitudinous personality tests available, but they tend to fall into two basic categories. There are the pencil-and-paper, self-report variety in which a person answers direct questions, and his answers are judged in various ways as normal or abnormal. The second type of personality test is the "projective technique" which calls for an interpretation of a picture or a design of some sort. The Rorschach or "ink-blot" test is a classic example of this. Another projective technique is to request the drawing of a person, a house, or a tree. There are many tests of this type available to the schools, and unfortunately, some teachers delight in using them.

Projective techniques assume that a person interprets or "colors" everything he does according to his mental state. This is probably true, but the problem lies in objectively "scoring" the projection. The "score" may actually be an interpretation (or projection) of the mental state of the person administering the test. So what does the score mean? Following the rationale of projection, an *objective* projective technique is a contradiction of terms.

Can we challenge test scores in school records? Technically, no. Test scores are factual material which cannot be challenged. But, if you feel that inappropriate education is being given to your child because of erroneous test scores, you can insist that better, more reliable tests be given to Johnnie. For example, if the school has placed Johnnie in a so-called "slow learner" group or a "career education" group or any other euphemistically labeled group which means "low ability," you might choose to question this placement. If the placement is based on a *group* intelligence test, you should ask that an individual test be given to Johnnie by a competent clinician. No child's placement in a special group should be based on only a group test. Educational placement is much too important for Johnnie's future to be based on tests which are invalid for him.

What material can we challenge in the school records then? The Right to Privacy amendment assures that opinions can be challenged and expunged. A teacher or administrator no longer can write derogatory comments or name-call Johnnie in school records. The school record cannot report that "Johnnie is a lazy, good-for-nothing brat." Because of this new law, very little of this kind of comment will continue to be written into school records; the law itself is a safeguard because there are legal procedures for dealing with defamation of this type.

Historically, schools have been most reluctant to reveal any test scores to parents, especially IQ scores. The school's official rationale for this reluctance has been that parents are not capable of understanding the scores. However, the schools have had another reason for concealing scores; if parents don't have any objective report of Johnnie's abilities or his achievements, the school cannot be held accountable for failing at its job. The new law makes accountability much easier to enforce.

Test scores permit parents to see what the school has and has not accomplished. The scores many times make it impossible for the school to blame the child or blame the parents for the child's lack of achievement. Responsibility for lack of achievement for a child with average or above average ability often lands neatly in the school's lap when objective test-score facts are known.

Parents who want information about any specific test should become familiar with Buros Mental Measurement Yearbooks. These reference volumes, which can be found in any library reference room, contain research reviews of all tests published in the United States.

8

A Final Word

A favorite target of vandalism is the schoolhouse. The cost of school repairs due to vandalism is astronomical. In 1974 alone, school vandalism cost taxpayers $500 millions. Obviously, the schools have done something to earn this kind of hostility. Studies done by child psychologists suggest a link between teacher abuse of children and school vandalism and attacks on teachers.

If we were granted the privilege of making one major change in America's schools, we would install the voucher system. In a country which has progressed and prospered because of the free-enterprise system, there is no better place for this than in our schools. The educational monopoly would no longer exist; students would not be prisoners of any one teacher or school system. Competition would spark improvement.

Under the voucher system, each child receives a ticket or tax-credit voucher for attendance to any school he chooses to attend, and a choice of teachers. The parents and the child choose a school and a specific teacher either in the neighborhood, as many would elect, or they have the option to choose any school, whether it is within their school district or in another school district, or even a private school. The voucher is presented to the school of choice and that school is then entitled to both state aid for the child and the money appropriated for each child in the local district from property taxes. Each child is entitled to the same amount of money for education, no matter how many children in the family. Transportation would be the family's responsibility if children chose to attend a school other than the neighborhood one. This would be a small price for parents to pay to insure appropriate education for their children.

This approach could also solve the problem of city school systems deteriorating because of the flight away from the city of those who can afford it, to the suburban schools. The system would work on an individual-choice basis as well as on a space-available basis, with preference given to those people living within the boundaries of the neighborhood the school serves. As the "better" schools became crowded, the others would become less crowded, and gradually the worst teachers would be laid off because of lack of customers, even those who were tenured. Eventually, the administrators in charge of the "good" schools would be given jurisdiction for reorganizing or reforming the schools which had been losing customers; and by this time, most of the worst educators would no longer have employment there. New teachers could be employed and trained by these "good" administrators. The existing teacher surplus would permit a wide choice of teachers to replace those whom the children and parents rejected. National institution of the voucher system would be the ace-trump card of Parent Prerogatives.

Index